NCERT
SOLUTIONS
with Chapterwise **Study Notes**

BIOLOGY 12th

Author

Manvi Sirohi
Anushri Sharma

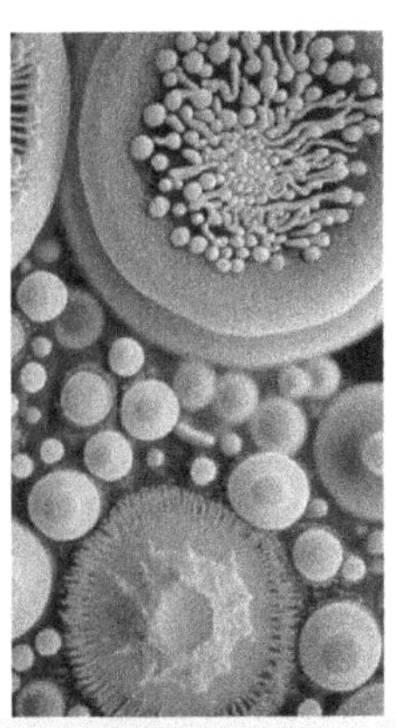

ARIHANT PRAKASHAN (Series), MEERUT

All Rights Reserved

ॐ Administrative & Production Offices

Regd. Office

'Ramchhaya' 4577/15, Agarwal Road, Darya Ganj, New Delhi -110002
Tele: 011- 47630600, 43518550

ॐ Head Office

Kalindi, TP Nagar, Meerut (UP) - 250002
Tel: 0121-7156203, 7156204

ॐ Sales & Support Offices

Agra, Ahmedabad, Bengaluru, Bareilly, Chennai, Delhi, Guwahati, Hyderabad, Jaipur, Jhansi, Kolkata, Lucknow, Nagpur & Pune.

ॐ PRICE

ॐ PO No : TXT-XX-XXXXXXX-X-XX

Published by Arihant Publications (India) Ltd.

For further information about the books published by Arihant, log on to www.arihantbooks.com or e-mail at info@arihantbooks.com

Follow us on

Preface

Feeling the immense importance and value of NCERT books, we are presenting this book, having the **NCERT Exercises Solutions**. For the overall benefit of the students we have made this book unique in such a way that it presents not only solutions but also detailed explanations. Through these detailed and through explanations, students can learn the concepts which will enhance their thinking and learning abilities.

We have introduced some Additional Features with the solutions which are given below:

- **Explanatory Solutions** Along with the solutions to questions we have given all the points that tell how to approach to solve a problem. Here we have tried to cover all those loopholes which may lead to confusion. All formulae and hints are discussed in full detail.
- Simplest language ensuring a thorough understanding of each solution.
- Expertly crafted and clearly labeled illustrations.

Apart from all those who helped in the compilation of this book a special note of thanks to all. With the hope that this book will be of great help to the students, we wish great success to our readers.

Manvi Sirohi
Anushri Sharma

Contents

Sexual Reproduction in Flowering Plants

CHAPTER 01

Important Points

01 All flowering plants (angiosperm) show sexual reproduction. In flowers, the male reproductive organ; **androecium** consists of **stamens** and female reproductive organ; **gynoecium** consist of **pistil.**

02 **Stamens** are the **male reproductive structures.** Each stamen has two parts :

(i) **Filament** A long slender stalk that supports the anther.

(ii) **Anther** A terminal, bilobed structure.

An angiosperm anther is **bilobed** and dithecous, with a groove separating the theca. Its transverse section shows a tetragonal structure with four microsporangia, two in each lobe.

03 **Structure of Microsporangium** A microsporangium is circular in transverse section, with four wall layers: epidermis, endothecium, middle layers (protection and dehiscence), and tapetum (nourishment). Tapetal cells are dense and often bi-nucleate. The center of microsporangia contains **sporogenous tissue.**

04 **Microsporogenesis**

(i) Each cell of sporogenous tissue is capable of giving rise to a microspore tetrad (cluster of four cells). Hence, each one is a potential pollen or microspore mother cell.

(ii) The process of formation of haploid microspores from diploid pollen mother cell through meiosis is called **microsporogenesis.**

05 Dehiscence of Anther As the anthers matures and dehydrate, it dehiscence and release thousands of microspores or pollen grains from each micro sporangium.

06 Structure of Pollen Grain Pollen grain represent the male gametophyte. They are generally spherical measuring about 25-50 micrometers in diameters.

It has two layers outer exine, made of sporopollenin (most-resistant organic material), has germ pore for pollen tube formation and inner intine (pectocellulosic nature)

07 Development of Male Gametophyte

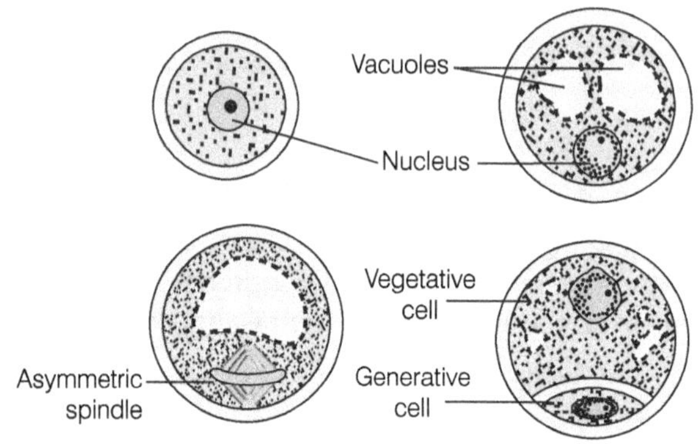

▲ Stages of a microspore maturing into a pollen grain

When the pollen grain is mature it contains two cells, vegetative cell and generative cell.

In many angiosperms, pollen grains are shed at the 2-celled stage. But in some species, pollen grains are shed at the 3-celled stage (one vegetative cell and two germ cells).

08 Pollen Allergies Pollen from many species, including Parthenium, causes allergies and respiratory issues like asthma and bronchitis.

Uses of Pollen Grains Pollens are rich in nutrients, therefore is, used as food supplements in tablets and syrups, claimed to boost performance of athletes and **race horse.**

09 **The Pistil** (gynoecium) It is the female reproductive part of the flower. A flower may consist of single pistil, (monocarpellary) or more than one pistils (multicarpellary).

When more than one pistils are present they may be :
  (i) fused together—syncarpous pistils
  (ii) free—apocarpous pistils.

10 **Each Pistil has three Parts** A pistil comprises of stigma (pollen landing), style (slender stalk), and ovary (basal bulge with locule and placenta). Megasporangia, or ovules, arise from the placenta.

11 **Structure of Megasporangium** A typical angiosperm ovule is attached to the placenta by a stalk called the funicle, with the hilum being the point of attachment. It has protective integuments, which encircle the nucellus except at the micropyle (tip) and chalaza (base). The nucellus contains reserve food and houses the embryo sac, formed from a megaspore.

12 **Megasporogenesis**
  (i)   The process of formation of megaspore from the megaspore mother cell is called megasporogenesis.
  (ii) A single megaspore mother cell is differentiated in the micropylar region of the nucellus and divides meiotically to form four haploid **megaspores.**
  (iii) Three of the megaspores degenerate and one remains functional, which develops into embryo sac or the **female gametophyte,** called monosporic dovelopment.

13 **Process of Formation of Embryo Sac/Female Gametophyte** The nucleus of the functional megaspore undergoes mitosis resulting in 2-nuclei that move to the opposite poles forming 2-nucleate embryo sac. Two more sequential mitotic free nuclear divisions result in 8-nucleate stage of the embryo sac.

Generally six of the 8-nuclei are surface by cell wall and remaining 2-celled polar nuclei lie free in the large central cell.

14 **Characteristic Distribution of Cells in the Embryo Sac**

The embryo sac has three cells at the micropylar end (egg apparatus two synergids with filiform apparatus and one egg cell), three antipodal cells at the chalazal end, and a central cell with two polar nuclei, making it 7-celled and 8-nucleate, called polygonum type.

15 Pollination It is the mechanism of transfer of pollen grains from anther to the stigma. Agents that bring about pollination are abiotic (water and air) or biotic (animals).

Depending on the source of pollen, pollination is of different types

(i) **Autogamy**

(a) Pollen goes to the stigma of same flower.

(b) Some plants such as *Oxalis, Commelina* and *Viola* produce two types of flowers- chasmogamous flowers which are similar to flowers of other species with exposed anthers and stigma and cleistogamous flowers which do not open at all.

(ii) **Geitonogamy** Transfer of pollen grains from anther to the stigma of another flower of the same plant. It is functionally cross pollination but genetically autogamy.

(iii) **Xenogamy** It involves transfer of pollen grains from anther to the stigma of a different plant.

16 Agents of Pollination

(i) **Abiotic** (wind and water)

(a) **Characterstics of flowers pollinated by wind** Wind pollination involves light, non-sticky pollen, exposed stamens, and large stigmas to trap airborne pollen. Flowers often have a single ovule per ovary and are clustered, as seen in grasses and corn.

(b) **Characteristics of flowers pollinated by water** In water-pollinated species, male gametes are carried by water currents, with pollen often protected by a mucilaginous covering.

(ii) **Biotic** (Animals)

- Flowers are large, colourful, fragrant and rich in nectar, so they attract insects bees, butterfly, birds and wasps.

- Some flowers provide a safe place for laying eggs in the flower., *e.g., Yucca, Amorphophallus.*

17 Outbreeding Devices Continued self-pollination result in inbreeding depression. Hence, flowering plants have developed many devices to discourage self-pollination and to encourage cross-pollination which are as follows :

(i) **Avoiding synchronisation** In some species, pollen release and stigma receptivity are not synchronised.

(ii) **Arrangement of anthers and stigma at different position** So that the pollen cannot come in contact with the stigma of the same flower.

(iii) **Self incompatibility** This is a genetic mechanism that prevents self fertilisation and promotes cross pollination.

(iv) **Production of unisexual flower** In several species such as papaya, male and female flowers are present on different plants. This condition prevents both autogamy and geitonogamy.

18 Pollen-Pistil Interaction

Pollen-pistil interaction refers to the process where pollen grain lands on the stigma of the pistil, triggering a series of biochemical events that allow the pollen tube to grow down the style to reach the ovary for fertilisation.

A plant breeder can manipulate pollen-pistil interaction, even in incompatible pollination to get desired hybrids.

19 Artificial Hybridisation in crop breeding involves **emasculation** (removal) of anthers and **bagging** (covering flowers to prevent contamination) to ;ensure only desired pollen is used. For bisexual flowers, emasculation is followed by bagging, and pollen is applied when the stigma is receptive. In unisexual flowers, bagging is done before flowering, and pollination occurs when the stigma is ready.

20 Double Fertilisation During double fertilisation, one male gamete fuses with the egg cell to form a zygote, while the other fuses with two polar nuclei to form a **triploid primary endosperm nucleus (PEN).** The zygote becomes the embryo, and the PEN develops into the endosperm.

21 Post-Fertilisation Events All those events that occurs in a flower after fertilisation are collectively termed as post fertilisation events.

The post-fertilisation events includes. Development of endosperm, Development of embryo, Maturation of ovules into seed, Maturation of ovary into fruits.

22 **Endosperm Development**

   (i) The primary endosperm cell divides repeatedly and forms a triploid endosperm tissue.

  (iii) During endosperm development, the PEN undergoes successive nuclear divisions to give rise to free nuclei. This stage of endosperm development is called free-nuclear endosperm. Then the cell wall formation occurs and the endosperm becomes cellular *e.g.,* coconut (made up of thousands of nuclei).

23 **Embryo Development** The embryo develops at the micropylar end of the embryo sac, where the zygote is located. After some endosperm is formed, the zygote divides, ensuring the developing embryo has a steady supply of nutrition. In both monocots and dicots, early embryogenesis is similar. Dicot embryos have an embryonal axis, two cotyledons, epicotyl (with plumule), hypocotyl, and radicle. Monocot embryos, like those in grasses, have one cotyledon (scutellum), with the radicle enclosed by coleorrhiza and the epicotyl protected by coleoptile.

24 **Seed** It is the fertilised ovule formed inside the fruit. It consists of seed(s) coat (hardened ovule integuments), cotyledon(s) and an embryonal axis.

Two types of mature seeds are

   (i) **Non-albuminous** in which endosperm is completely consumed during embryo development, usually found in dicot plants, *e.g.,* pea and groundnut.

  (ii) **Albuminous** that retain part of endosperm as it is not completely consumed during embryo development, usually found in monocot plants, *e.g.* wheat, castor maize and barley.

      In some seeds, remnants of nucellus are persistant which is called perisperm, *e.g.,* black pepper and beet root.

25 **Dormancy** As the seed matures, its water content get reduced and the seed becomes dry. The general metabolic activities of embryo slow down and the embryo may enter into a state of inactivity called **dormancy.**

26 **Fruits** ovary develops into fruit and ovule matures into seeds. The wall of ovary becomes wall of fruit, *i.e.* pericarp.

The fruits may be fleshy as in guava, orange and mango or may be dry, as in groundnut and mustard.

Fruits are of two types namely
  (i) **True fruits** They are formed from the ovary of flower. *e.g.* mango and maize
  (ii) **False fruits** In these, parts of the flower other than the ovary like thalamus also contribute to the formation of fruit. *e.g.* apple, strawberry and cashew.

  In some species like banana, the fruits develop without fertilisation. Such fruits are called parthenocarpic fruits.

27 **Advantages of Seed**
  (i) Seeds have better adaptive strategies for dispersal to new habitats and help the species to colonise in other areas.
  (ii) They have sufficient food reserves to nourish young seedlings until, they are capable of photosynthesis on their own.
  (iii) Being products of sexual reproduction, they generate new genetic combinations, leading to variations.
  (iv) Dehydration and dormancy of mature seeds are crucial for their storage, allowing them to be used as food throughout the year and to grow crops in the next season.

28 **Apomixis** refers to the phenomenon of formation of seeds without fertilisation, *e.g.*, asteraceae and grasses.

29 Polyembryony is the phenomenon of formation of more than one embryo in the seed, *e.g.*, *Citrus* and mango.

Exercises

Question 1 Name the parts of an angiosperm flower in which development of male and female gametophyte take place.

Sol. In an angiosperm flower, development of male gametophyte takes place in pollen sac of the anther while the development of female gametophyte takes place in the nucellus of ovule.

Question 2 Differentiate between microsporogenesis and megasporogenesis. Which type of cell division occurs during these events? Name the structures formed at the end of these two events.

Sol. Differences between microsporogenesis and megasporogenesis are as follows.

S.N.	Microsporogenesis	Megasporogenesis
1.	It is the process of formation of haploid microspores (pollen grains) from diploid pollen mother cell through the meiosis.	It is the process of formation of haploid megaspores from diploid megaspore mother cell through the meiosis.
2.	The microspore mother cell first forms a tetrad (four cells), which dissociate from each other to form four functional pollen grains.	The megaspore mother cell forms four cells.Out of which only one megaspore is functional and develops into embryo sac, while other three degenerate.
3.	It occurs inside the pollen sac of the anther.	It occurs inside the ovule.

Both the events involves the process of meiosis or reductional division. At the end of microsporogenesis haploid microspores are formed whereas in megasporogenesis, haploid megaspore in formed.

Question 3 Arrange the following terms in the correct developmental sequence
Pollen grain, sporogenous tissue, microspore tetrad, pollen mother cell, male gametes.

Sol. The correct developmental sequence is as follows :

   (i) Sporogenous tissue   (ii) Pollen mother cell

  (iii) Microspore tetrad   (iv) Pollen grains

   (v) Male gametes

Question 4 With a neat, labelled diagram, describe the parts of a typical angiosperm ovule.

Sol. The labelled diagram of a typical ovule of angiosperm is as follows

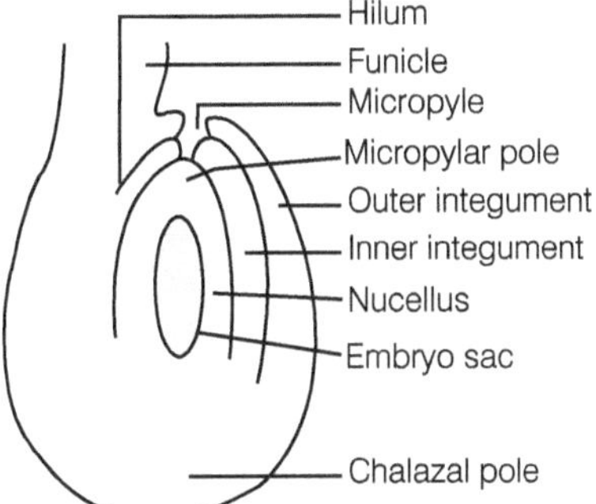

A diagrammatic view of a typical anatropous ovule

Description

An ovule has following parts

(i) **Attachment points**

Funicle is the stalk that attaches the ovule to placenta.

Hilum is the point, where funicle is attached to the ovule body.

(ii) **Integuments** Integuments are one or two outer layers, surrounding the ovule that provides protection to the developing embryo.

(iii) **Chalaza** Basal part of the ovule lies opposite to **micropyle.**

(iv) **Micropyle** A pore like structure on one side of the ovule, where integuments are absent is called **micropyle.**

(v) **Nucellus** A mass of cells that is enclosed within the integuments is called nucellus. Cells of nucellus have abundant reserves of food material.

(vi) **Embryo sac/ female gametophyte** It is located with in the nucellus. An ovule generally has a single embryo sac formed from the megaspore.

Question 5 What is meant by monosporic development of female gametophyte?

Sol. The method of embryo sac formation from a single megaspore is called monosporic development. In most flowering plants, a single megaspore mother cell present at the micropylar pole of the nucellus region of the ovule undergo meiosis to produce four haploid megaspore. Out of these four megaspores, only one megaspore is functional while the other three degenerate.

Question 6 With a neat diagram explain the 7-celled, 8-nucleate nature of the female gametophyte.

Sol.

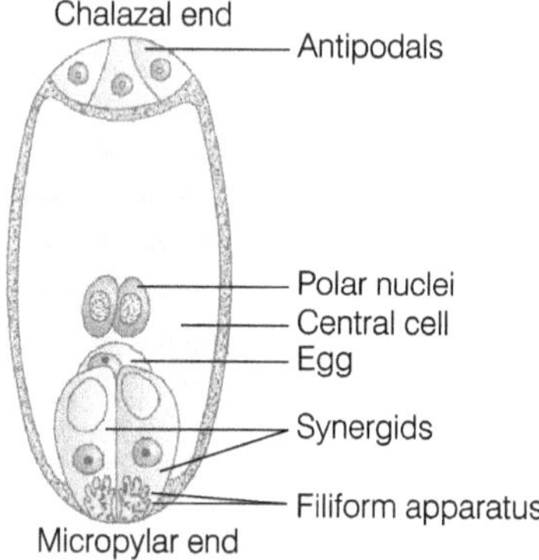

A diagrammatic representation of the mature embryo sac

Explanation The nucleus of the functional megaspore undergoes mitosis resulting in 2-nuclei that move to two opposite poles forming 2-nucleate embryo sac. Two more sequential mitotic nuclear divisions result in 4-nucleate and later 8-nucleate stages of the embryo sac. These division are free nuclear. After the 8 nucleate stage, cell walls are laid down leading to the organisation of female gametophyte or embryo sac.

Six of the 8-nuclei are bound by cell wall and the remaining 2 polar nuclei lie below the egg apparatus in the large central cell.

Distribution of cells within the embryo sac

Three cells are grouped together at the micropylar end and constitute the egg apparatus, which consists of two synergids and one egg cell.

Three cells at the chalazal end are called antipodals. The large central cell has 2-polar nuclei. Thus, a typical angiosperm embryo sac at maturity is 7-celled, but 8-nucleated.

Question 7 What are chasmogamous flowers? Can cross-pollination occur in cleistogamous flowers? Give reasons for your answer.

Sol. Chasmogamous flowers are open flowers and have exposed anthers and stigma. Cross-pollination cannot occur in cleistogamous flowers as they don't open at all. Also, their anthers and stigma lie close to each other. Hence, they only produce seeds through self-pollination.

Question 8 Mention two strategies evolved to prevent self-pollination in flowers.

Sol. Two strategies evolved to prevent self-pollination are :
  (i) Pollen release and stigma receptivity is not synchronised. (Dichogamy)
  (ii) Anthers and stigma are placed at such positions that pollen doesn't reach stigma.

Question 9 What is self-incompatibility? Why does self-pollination not lead to seed formation in self-incompatible species?

Sol. Self-incompatibility is a genetic mechanism to prevent self pollen from fertilising the ovules by inhibiting pollen germination or pollen tube growth in the pistil. So, it does not lead to seed formation.

Question 10 What is bagging technique? How is it useful in a plant breeding programme?

Sol. Bagging is a technique of covering the female plant with butter paper to prevent stigma from the contamination with undesired pollen. This is useful in plant breeding programme as it ensures that pollen grains of only desirable plants are used for fertilisation, leading to the development of desired plant variety. It also prevents damage by animals.

Question 11 What is triple fusion? Where and how does it take place? Name the nuclei involved in triple fusion.

Sol. Triple fusion refers to the process of fusion of one male gamete and two polar nuclei in the central cell of embryo sac of angiosperms to form primary-triploid endosperm nucleus. It takes place in the embryo sac.

The 3-nuclei that are involved in triple fusion are one male gamete and 2-polar nuclei of the central cell.

Question 12 Why do you think the zygote is dormant for sometime in a fertilised ovule?

Sol. The zygote is dormant in fertilised ovule for sometime because it waits for the endosperm to form. The endosperm serves as the source of nutrition for the developing embryo and after the formation of the endosperm, further development of the embryo from the zygote begins.

Question 13 Differentiate between

(i) Hypocotyl and epicotyl   (ii) Coleoptile and coleorhiza

(iii) Integument and testa   (iv) Perisperm and pericarp

Sol.   (i) Hypocotyl is the cylindrical portion below the level of cotyledons, terminating at its lower end in the radical or root tip.

Epicotyl is the portion of embryonal axis above the level of cotyledons, which terminates with the plumule or stem tip.

(ii) Coleoptile is a hollow foliar structure enclosing the shoot apex and few leaf primordia. Coleorhiza is an undifferentiated sheath enclosing the radical and root cap.

(iii) Integument is thin protective covering of ovules and the cells involved are living. Testa is thick outer protective covering of the seed and the cells involved are dead.

(iv) Perisperm is diploid residual, persistent nucellus.

Pericarp refers to the wall of fruit developed from the wall of ovary.

Question 14 Why is apple called a false fruit? Which part(s) of the flower forms the fruit?

Sol. Apple is a false fruit because in this fruit formation accessory floral parts are used (such as thalamus). Mainly ovary, the basal part of carpel forms fruit after fertilisation.

Question 15 What is meant by emasculation? When and why does a plant breeder employ this technique?

Sol. Emasculation is the process of removal of anthers, from the bisexual flower before dehiscence. Plant breeder employs this technique to prevent contamination of stigma with the undesired pollen as well as chances of self pollination. This is useful in artificial hybridisation, where desired pollen is required to develop the desired plants variety.

Question 16 If one can induce parthenocarpy through the application of growth substances, which fruits would you select to induce parthenocarpy and why?

Sol. Parthenocarpic fruits develop without fertilisation and are seedless. Hence, fleshy fruits like oranges, lemons, watermelon, etc. could be selected for inducing the parthenocarpy because seedless variety of these fruits would be much appreciated by the consumers. This is also important in first processing industry and first grown in green house, where natural pollinators are not available.

Question 17 Explain the role of tapetum in the formation of pollen grain wall.

Sol. Tapetum is the innermost layer of the microsporangium and provides nourishment to the developing pollen grains. It produces the exine layer of the pollen grains, which is composed of the sporopollenin, the most resistant organic material. During microsporogenesis, the cells of tapetum produce various enzymes, hormones, amino acids and other nutritious material required for the development of pollen grains.

Question 18 What is apomixis and what is its importance?

Sol. Apomixis is the of mechanism of production of seeds without fertilisation. It is a form of asexual reproduction that mimics sexual reproduction.

Thus, the plants that grow from these seeds are identical to the mother plant.

The importance of apomixis are as follows.

(i) It is a cost effective method for producing seeds.

(ii) It helps to prevent the loss of specific characters in a hybrid.

DIKSHA APP Questions

☐ Multiple Choice Questions

Q.1 Perisperm refers to the following

(a) remains of endosperm.
(b) residual persistent nucellus in the seed.
(c) remains of integuments.
(d) remains of thalamus.

Sol. (b) The perisperm refers to the residual persistent nucellus in the seed. It is a layer of nutritive tissue that surrounds the embryo of a seed. Perisperm is present in seeds such as black pepper and beet root.

☐ Very Short Answer Type

Q.1 Define a typical angiosperm anther.

Sol. A typical angiospermic anther is bilobed with each lobe having two theca, *i.e.*, they are dithecous. A longitudinal groove runs lengthwise through, it separating the two theca. The anther has a four-sided (tetragonal) structure consisting of four microsporangia located at the corners, which develop further and become pollen sacs that are packed with pollen grains.

Q.2 Suggest one method to preserve pollen grains. Why do we store pollengrains?

Sol. Cryopreservation stored pollengrains can be used as pollen banks in crop breeding programmes.

Q.3 What do you mean by pollen viability?

Sol. The period for which the pollen grains can retain the ability to germinate is known as pollen viability.

Q.4 Pollengrains are considered as food supplements, Comment on it.

Sol. Pollengrains are rich in nutrients and it will enhance the metabolism of living organism. Hence, they are considered as food supplements.

Q.5 Differentiate between funicle and hilum.

Sol. The funicle is the stalk that attaches the ovule to the placenta, while the hilum is the point where the funicle connects to the ovule,

Q.6 Write down the alternative name for angiosperm ovule.

Sol. The alternative name of the angiospermic ovule is "megasporangium."

☐ Short Answer Type

Q.1 Pistil can identify a right type of pollen grain from a wrong type. Is it possible?

Sol. Yes, it is possible as the pistil has the ability to recognise the pollen due to the presence of a continuous dialogue between pollen grain and the pistil. This dialogue is mediated by chemical components of the pollen interacting with those of the pistil.

Q.2 Name an out breeding device which prevents both autogamy and geitonogamy.

Sol. The out breeding device that prevents both autogamy and geitonogamy is dioecious condition where the male and female flowers are present on different plants, *i.e.* each plant is either male or female, example papaya.

Q.3 What do you mean by out breeding devices?

Sol. Flowering plants have developed many devices to discourage self-pollination and to encourage cross-pollination, such devices are known as out breeding devices.

Q.4 Name the floral rewards a biotic agent is getting from a flower?

Sol. Biotic agents get various rewards from a flower which include nectar, pollen grains, space to lay eggs, etc. In exchange of these rewards biotic agents helps in the transfer of pollen from one place to another(pollination) .

Q.5 How the pollen grains are preserved in the water pollinated species?

Sol. In most of the water-pollinated species, the pollen grains are protected from wetting by a mucilaginous covering on them.

Q.6 What is the importance of pollination in angiosperm?

Sol. Pollination is important in angiosperms because it enables sexual reproduction, leading to the fomation of seeds and fruits. Pollination also promotes genetic diversity which prevents inbreeding depression.

Q.7 Bryophytes and pteridophytes distribution is limited. Give Reason

Sol. Bryophytes and pteridophytes distribution is limited because they need water as a medium for the transport of motile male gametes for fertilisation.

Q.8 What is geitonogamy? It is considered as xenogamy as well as autogamy. Give reason

Sol. The transfer of pollen grains from the anther to the stigma of another flower of the same plant is known as geitonogamy. It is also considered as xenogamy because a pollinating agent is required for pollination. It is considered as autogamy because pollen grains come from the same plant.

Q.9 Name the type of flower, which promote xenogamy and autogamy.

Sol. Flowers which promote xenogamy are chasmogamous flowers.

(a) The type of flowers which promote xenogamy are chasmogamous flowers. These flowers have exposed anthers and stigma. In such flowers genetically different types of pollen grains are brought to the stigma thus increasing genetic variation and promoting xenogamy.

(b) The type of flowers which promote autogamy are cleistogamous flowers. These flowers do not open at all and thus ensure autogamy leading to a decrease in the genetic variation in plant.

Q.10 What is filiform apparatus? Write down it's function.

Sol. The finger like projections found in synergids are known as filiform apparatus. It's function is to guide the pollen tube into the embryo sac for the fertilisation activity.

Q.11 What do you mean by monosporic development of embryo sac?

Sol. Embryosac develops from a single functional megaspore, (out of four megaspores) this type of embryo sac development is known as monosporic development of embryo sac.

Q.12 Write down any two advantages of seeds to an angiosperm.

Sol. The two advantages of seeds of an angiosperm are listed below.

(a) Seeds are the product of sexual reproduction, so it brings variation.

(b) Seeds can store reserve food materials for the developing seedlings.

Human Reproduction

Important Points

01 Humans are sexually reproducing and viviparous organisms. The reproductive events in humans include gametogenesis, insemination, fertilisation, implantation, gestation, parturition.

02 **Male Reproductive System** The male reproductive system consists of a pair of testes, accessory ducts, accessory glands and external genitalia which are discused below.

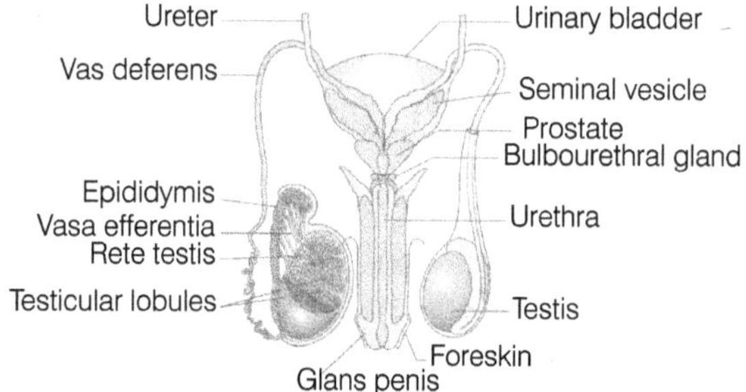

▲ Diagrammatic view of male reproductive system
(part of testes is open to show inner details)

(i) **Testes** These are the primary male sex organs.

They are located in the scrotum, which maintains temperature 2-3 degree lower than body temperature essential for sperm production. Each testes contains seminiferous tubules where sperms are produced and is lined with two types of cells, male germs cells (spermatogonia) and Sertoli cells. The interstitial spaces outside the seminiferous tubules contain Leydig cells, which synthesise and secrete androgens.

(ii) **Accessory Ducts** includes **rete testis, vasa efferentia, epididymis** and **vas deferens** which helps to store and transport sperm from testes to outside, through the urethra during ejaculation.

(iii) **Accessory Glands** It include the seminal vesicles, prostate, and bulbourethral glands, which secrets seminal plasma rich in fructose, calcium, and enzymes, aiding in lubrication and sperm nourishment.

(iv) **Penis** It is the male external genitalia. It is made up of a special erectile tissue to help insemination.

03 Female Reproductive System The female reproductive system consists of a pair of ovaries, accessory ducts, a pair of mammary glands and external genitalia which are discussed below.

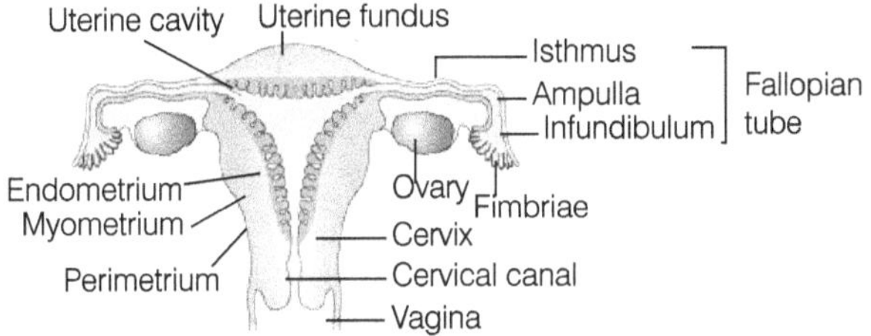

▲ Diagrammatic sectional view of the female reproductive system

(i) **Ovaries** These are the primary female sex organs and are located one on each side of the lower abdomen. They are responsible for producing the female gamete (ovum) and several steroid hormones (ovarian hormones).

(ii) **The Accessory Ducts** The Fallopian tubes, uterus and vagina constitute the accessory ducts.

- Each Fallopian tube extends from ovary to the uterus. The part closer to the ovary is funnel-shaped called **infundibulum**. Edges of infundibulum have finger-like projections called **fimbrae** that help in collecting ovum after ovulation. The infundibulum leads to the **ampulla** which in turn leads to **isthmus** which open into uterus.

- **Uterus** It is a muscular chamber, supported by ligaments attached to the pelvis wall. It opens into vagina through a narrow cervix.

- Uterine wall has three layers of tissue *i.e.,* perimetrium, Myometrium and endometrium.

Vagina It is a muscular elastic tube that connects the external genitalia to the uterus, serving as the passage way for menstrual flow and child birth. The vagina opens through an aperture called vaginal orifice.

04 **Female External Genitalia** mons pubis, labia majora, labia minora, hymen and clitoris.

05 **Mammary Glands** These are paired structures that contain **glandular** and **fatty tissues.**

Function Secretion and storage of milk and colostrum (a fluid rich in proteins, lactose and immunity enhancing antibodies). Bartholin's gland and Skene's gland are also present to help in lubrication and prevent spread of bacteria.

06 **Gametogenesis** The process by which diploid germ cells undergo meiosis to form haploid gametes. Two processes of gametogenesis are spermatogenesis and oogenesis.

Spermatogenesis It is a process of formation of sperm, through meiotic division from germ cells present in testis. Sperm formation depends on hormones, specifically LH, FSH and testosterone.

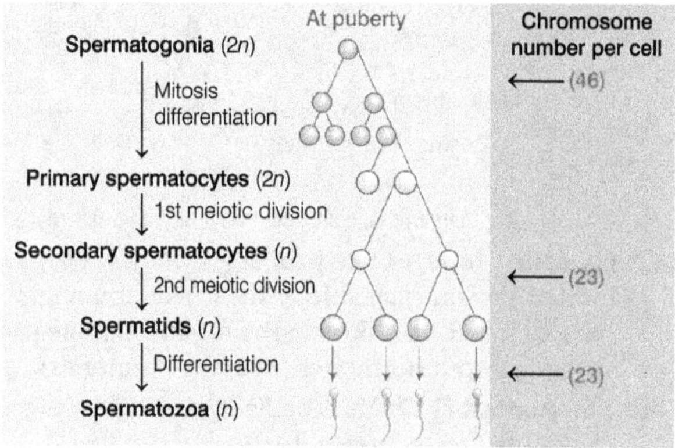

▲ Schematic view of spermatogenesis

Hormones in Spermatogenesis

Gn RH (Gonadotropin-releasing hormone) Released by the hypothalamus, it stimulates the anterior pituitary to release LH and FSH.

LH (Luteinising Hormone) Stimulates leydig cells in the testis to produce testosterone.

Testosterone Essential for the development and maturation of sperm cells and maintaing male reproductive tissues.

FSH (Follicle-Stimulating Hormone) Acts on sertoli cells in the seminiferous tubules to support spermatogenesis and sperm maturation.

07 Sperm Cell A normal human sperm has three parts :

   (i) **Head** contains haploid nucleus with enzyme rich cap called acrosome. Acrosome contain hydrolytic enzymes, which helps to dissolve outer cover of ovum.

   (ii) **Middle piece** has numerous mitochondria to supply energy to facilitate quick movement of the sperm.

   (iii) **Tail** has a core of microtubules for fast movement of sperm up through the female reproductive tract to ensure fertilisation.

08 Oogenesis It is the process of formation of female gametes (oocyte) through meiotic division of germ cells, present in the ovary.

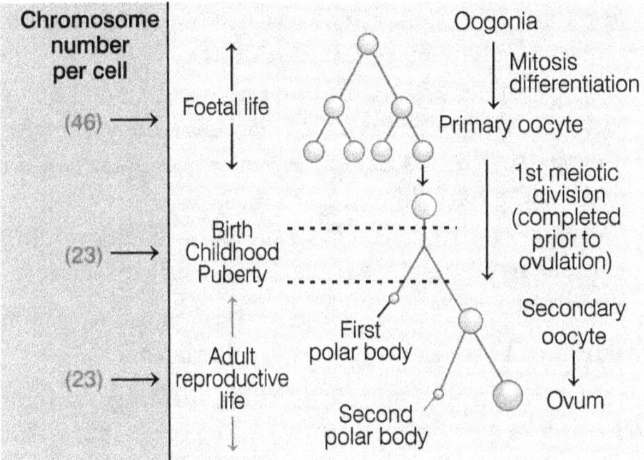

▲ Diagrammatic view of phases in oogenesis

09 Menstrual Cycle The reproductive cycle of female primates is called **menstrual cycle**. It starts at puberty, called menarche. It is repeated at an interval of 28-29 days.

10 The Events of Menstrual Cycle

   (i) **Menstrual phase** The absence of fertilisation results in the breakdown of endometrial lining with sloughed off endometrial tissue, expelled out through the vaginal canal. This is known as **menstrual flow** and may last for 3-6 days.

   (ii) **Follicular phase** Primary follicles in the ovary grow to become fully mature **Graafian follicles.**

     At the same time, the endometrium starts proliferating due to secretion of LH and FSH, from anterior pituitary.

(iii) **Ovulation Phase** Rapid secretion of LH leading to its maximum level during the mid-cycle called LH surge induces rupture of Graafian follicle and thereby the release of ovum (ovulation).

(iv) **Luteal Phase** After ovulation, the remaining parts of Graafian follicle transform into **corpus luteum**, a glandular structure. It secretes large amount of **progesterone**, which help in maintenance of endometrium.

A well-developed endometrium will ensure implantation and later events of pregnancy.

11 Fertilisation It is the process of fusion of sperm and ovum.

  (i) During sexual intercourse the semen is released from penis into the vagina (insemination) and the sperm travels to the fallopian tube, where fertilisation takes place.

 (ii) The sperm penetrates the zona pellucida using acrosomal enzymes which induces the secondary oocyte to complete meiosis-II. This results in the formation of a second polar body and a haploid ovum.

(iii) Fertilisation process ends when haploid sperm nucleus and haploid ovum nucleus fuses. This results in the formation of a **diploid zygote**.

12 Formation of Early Embryo and Implantation

The zygote undergoes mitotic division, forming blastomeres that develop into a morula. The morula transforms into a blastocyst, with an outer trophoblast layer and an inner cell mass. The blastocyst attaches to the endometrium, leading to implantation and the onset of pregnancy.

13 Pregnancy Implantation of zygote in the uterus leads to pregnancy. It lasts for 38 weeks from the time of fertilisation.

14 Placenta is a structural and functional unit between developing embryo and maternal body that facilitates the exchange of substances between the mother and the developing baby, without intermingling of their blood streams.

  (i) Placenta also acts as endocrine tissue and secretes **human chorionic gonadotropin, human placental lactogen, oestrogen and progesterone.**

 (ii) In later pregnancy period, relaxin hormone is also produced that help in softening and widening of the cervix as well as loosening muscles and ligaments in the pelvis.

15 Embryonic and Foetal Development
  (i) After implantation, inner cell mass differentiates into ectoderm (outer layer), mesoderm (middle layer) and endoderm (inner layer).
  (ii) These three layers give rise to all tissues and organs of the adult human body.

16 Parturition The process of childbirth is called **parturition**, which is induced by a complex neuroendocrine mechanism involving cortisol, oestrogen and oxytocin.

17 Lactation Mammary glands differentiate during pregnancy and secrete milk (lactation) after childbirth

The fluid produced during initial few days of lactation is called **colostrum**. It contains important antibodies, essential to develop resistance in the newborn baby.

Exercises

Question 1 Fill in the blanks.

    (a) Humans reproduce .... (asexually/sexually)

    (b) Humans are .... (oviparous/viviparous/ovoviviparous)

    (c) Fertilisation is ...... in humans. (external/internal)

    (d) Male and female gametes are .... (diploid/haploid)

    (e) Zygote is .... (diploid/haploid)

    (f) The process of release of ovum from a mature follicle is called ....

    (g) Ovulation is induced by a hormone called .... .

    (h) The fusion of male and female gametes is called .... .

    (i) Fertilisation takes place in ....

    (j) Zygote divides to form ...... which is implanted in uterus.

    (k) The structure which provides vascular connection between foetus and uterus is called ....

Sol.

(a) Sexually	(b) Viviparous
(c) Internal	(d) Haploid
(e) Diploid	(f) Ovulation.
(g) Luteinising Hormone (LH)	(h) Fertilisation
(i) Oviduct (ampulla-isthmus junction)	(j) Blastocyst
(k) Placenta.	

Question 2 Draw a labelled diagram of male reproductive system.

Sol.

Diagrammatic view of male reproductive system

Question 3 Draw a labelled diagram of female reproductive system.

Sol.

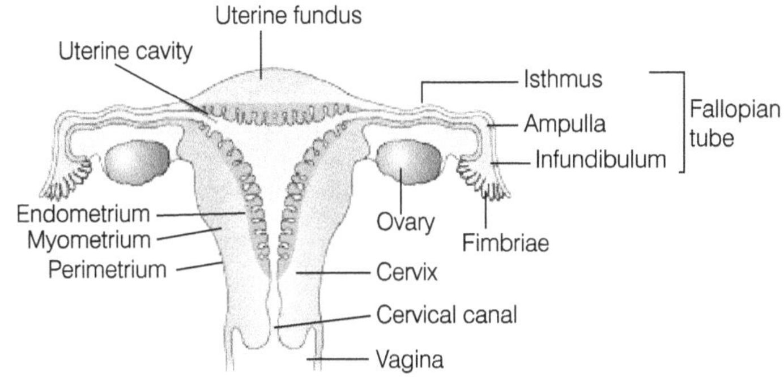

Diagrammatic sectional view of the female reproductive system

Question 4 Write two major functions of each testis and ovary.

Sol. Two major functions of ovary are as follows :

(i) Production of ova (female gamete)

(ii) Production of female sex hormones, *e.g.,* oestrogen and progesterone.

Two major functions of testis are as follows :

(i) Production of sperm (male gamete)

(ii) Production of male sex hormones, *e.g.,* testosterone.

Question 5 Describe the structure of a seminiferous tubule.

Sol. Seminiferous tubules are highly coiled structures within the testicular lobules of testes. These are lined on the inside by germinal epithelium. It has two types of cells

(i) Male germ cells called spermatogonia that undergo meiotic division to form sperm cells.

(ii) Sertoli cells that provide nutrition and molecular signals to the developing spermatozoa.

Question 6 What is spermatogenesis? Briefly describe the process of spermatogenesis.

Sol. Spermatogenesis is the process of formation of mature male gametes, cells, from male germ cells.

(i) The germ cells called spermatogonia are present on the inside wall of the seminiferous tubules.

(ii) These cells are diploid and multiply by mitosis to increase in number.

(iii) Some of the spermatogonia undergo meiosis, they will be referred to as primary spermatocytes.

(iv) The primary spermatocyte completes first meiotic division, leading to formation of two equal, haploid cells called secondary spermatocytes. They have only 23 chromosomes, but they are still duplicate. Contain two sister chromatids.

(v) Each of the two secondary spermatocytes undergoes second meiotic division producing four haploid spermatids. Each has one copy of 23 chromosomes.

(vi) Spermatids transform into spermatozoa (sperm cells) by developing a head, neck, middle piece and a tail. This process is called spermiogenesis.

(vii) Sperm heads become embedded in the Sertoli cells.

(viii) Final release of sperms (spermiation) from seminiferous tubules is under the influence of hormonal and physiological factors.

Note   Remember in meiosis, there are two cell divisions, one after the other. In meiosis I, the homologous pair of chromosome separate into two haploid cells, while in meiosis-II, the sister chromotids of each chromosome are separated into four haploid cells. Hence, it results in the generation of four genetically unique haploid cells.

Summary of spermatogenesis

Diploid spermatogonia (germ cells in the seminiferous tubules) →

→ Primary spermatocytes First meiotic division → Two haploid spermatids

secondary spermatocytes → Second meiotic division → Four haploid spermatids

Question 7 Name the hormones involved in regulation of spermatogenesis.

Sol.   The hormones involved in the regulation of spermatogenesis are

(i) Gonadotropin Releasing Hormone (GnRH) — Released from hypothalamus and triggers release of FSH and LH from the pituitary gland.

(ii) Luteinising Hormone (LH) — Released from pituitory gland, acts on Leydig cells and stimulate testosterone production.

(iii) Follicle Stimulating Hormone (FSH)   — Released from pituitary gland and stimulate sperm production.

Question 8 Define spermiogenesis and spermiation.

Sol.   Spermiogenesis is the process of transformation of spermatids into fully developed sperm cells (or spermatozoa) with a head, neck, middle piece and a tail. Spermiation is the process of final release of sperm cells from the seminiferous tubules, under the influence of hormonal and physiological factors.

Question 9 Draw a labelled diagram of sperm.

Sol.

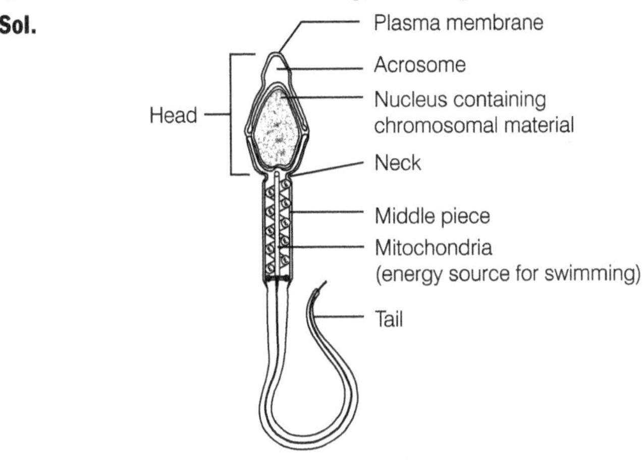

Structure of a sperm

Question 10 What are the major components of seminal plasma?

Sol. Major components of human seminal plasma are fructose, citric acid, fibrinogen, prostaglandins, mucus, lipids, buffering agents, proteolytic enzymes all coming from the secretions of

(i) epididymis

(ii) vas deferens

(iii) seminal vesicles

(iv) prostate

It may or may not contain sperm.

Question 11 What are the major functions of male accessory ducts and glands?

Sol. The male accessory ducts include rete testis, vasa efferentia, epididymis and vas deferens. The major functions of these ducts are storage and transport of sperms from testis to the outside through urethra.

The male accessory glands include seminal vesicle, prostate glands and bulbo-urethral glands. The major functions of these glands include secretion of seminal plasma, which is rich in fructose, calcium and certain enzymes.

Question 12 What is oogenesis? Give a brief account of oogenesis.

Sol. Oogenesis is the process of formation of mature female gametes (ova) from primordial germ cells.

(i) This process is initiated during embryonic developmental stage when about two million gamete mother cells (oogonia) are formed in each foetal ovary.

(ii) Oogonia undergo meiotic division, which gets arrested at prophase-I stage. They are referred to as primary oocytes.

(iii) Each of these gets covered with layers of granulosa cells and are then called primary follicle.

(iv) Many of the primary follicles degenerate from birth to puberty, leaving about 60000-80000 in each ovary at puberty.

(v) More layers of granulosa cells and an another theca layer surround it and now it is called secondary follicle. Theca layer is arranged as inner theca–interna and outer theca– externa.

(vi) Secondary follicle transforms into tertiary follicle that has a fluid filled cavity called antrum.

(vii) The primary oocyte within the tertiary follicle grows in size and completes its first meiotic division now.

(viii) This is an unequal division resulting in the formation of

(a) a large haploid cell (that keeps the majority of nutrient rich cytoplasm) called **secondary oocyte**.

(b) a tiny cell, with haploid nucleus and almost no cytoplasm called **first polar body**.

(ix) The tertiary follicle undergoes certain modifications and changes into a mature Graafian follicle

(x) Secondary oocyte forms a new membrane around it, called zona pellucida.

(xi) Under the influence of LH, the Graaffian follicle ruptures to release secondary oocyte from the ovary by a process called **ovulation**.

Summary of oogenesis

Oogonia → Meiosis-I initiated → Primary oocyte (arrested at prophase-I) → Granulosa layer builds → Primary follicle → More granulosa and theca layer added → Secondary follicle → Fluid filled cavity develops → Tertiary follicle → Primary oocyte completes meiosis-I → Secondary oocyte (haploid) + polar body → Tertiary follicle transforms to Graafian follicle → Zona pellucida builds around secondary oocyte → Graafian follicle ruptures → Secondary oocyte (ovum) released.

Meiosis-II will occur only at the time of penetration of sperm into the ovum.

Question 13 Draw a labelled diagram of a section through ovary.

Sol. Diagram of a section through ovary

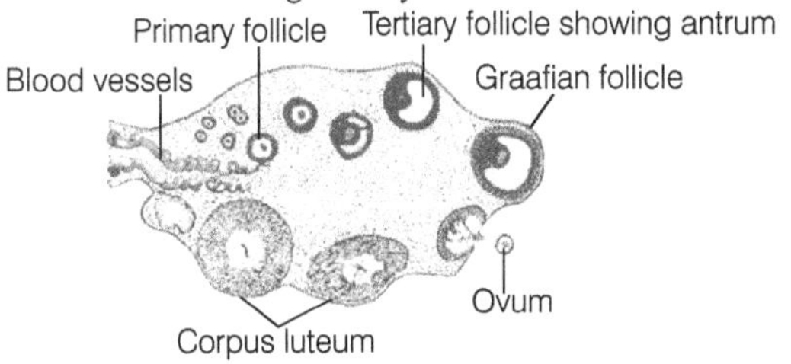

Diagrammatic section view of ovary

Question 14 Draw a labelled diagram of a Graafian follicle.

Sol. Diagram of Graaffian follicle

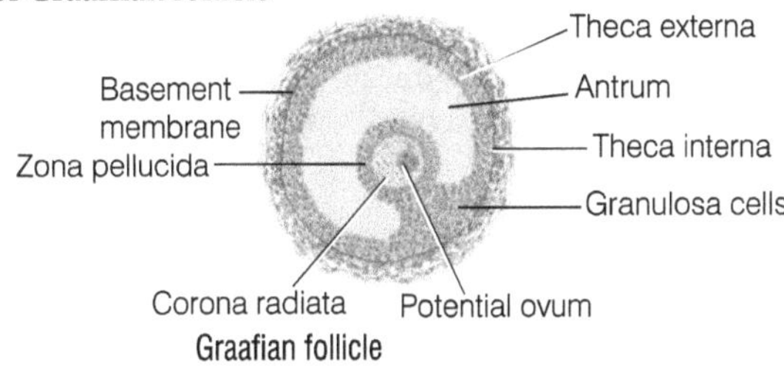

Graafian follicle

Question 15 Name the functions of the following

(a) Corpus luteum   (b) Endometrium   (c) Acrosome
(d) Sperm tail   (e) Fimbriae

Sol. The functions of the following :

(a) **Corpus luteum** secretes large amount of progesterone, which is essential for the maintenance of endometrium of the uterus.

(b) **Endometrium** is necessary for the implantation of the zygote, contributing towards formation of placenta and other events of pregnancy. In the absence of implantation, it undergo cyclic changes of growth and degeneration.

(c) **Acrosome** is filled with citric enzymes that help in dissolving the outer cover (zona pellucida) of the ovum and entry of sperm nucleus.

(d) **Sperm tail** facilitates motility to the sperm, essential for reaching to the ovum to fertilise it.

(e) **Fimbriae** are fingers-like projections at the end of Fallopian tubules that help in collection of the ovum after ovulation.

Question 16 Identify true/false statements. Correct each false statement to make it true.

(a) Androgens are produced by Sertoli cells.   (True/False)
(b) Spermatozoa get nutrition from Sertoli cells.   (True/False)

(c) Leydig cells are found in ovary.   (True/False)

(d) Leydig cells synthesise androgens.   (True/False)

(e) Oogenesis takes place in corpus luteum.   (True/False)

(f) Menstrual cycle ceases during pregnancy.   (True/False)

(g) Presence or absence of hymen is not a reliable indicator of virginity or sexual experience.   (True/False)

Sol. Identify true or false and correct if false

  (a) Androgens are produced by Sertoli cells.   (False)

      Correct: Androgens are produced by leydig cells.

  (b) Spermatozoa get nutrition from Sertoli cells.   (True)

  (c) Leydig cells are found in ovary.   (False)

      Correct: Leydig cells are found in testis

  (d) Leydig cells synthesise androgens.   (True)

  (e) Oogenesis takes place in corpus luteum.   (False)

      Correct: Oogenesis takes place in ovarian follicles ovary

  (f) Menstrual cycle ceases during pregnancy.   (True)

  (g) Presence or absence of hymen is not a reliable indicator of virginity or sexual experience.   (True)

Question 17 What is menstrual cycle? Which hormones regulate menstrual cycle?

Sol. Menstrual cycle refers to reproductive cycle that encompasses a series of changes occuring in reproductively active human females and other primates. The event repeats every 28/29 days in a cyclical fashion, hence it is called menstrual cycle. During each menstrual cycle, an oocyte matures and is released from the ovary towards Fallopian tubes. At the same time, the uterine endometrium prepares to receive and nourish the embryo, if fertilisation of this ovum takes place. However, in the absence of fertilisation, 50-100 mL of blood rich fluid out through the vaginal canal. This is known as menstrual flow. After this, once again the endometrium starts rebuilding, the ovulation will occur again and the same process follows in a time period of 28-29 days.

The hormones involved in the process are

  (i) **FSH, LH** stimulate growth of follicle and maturation of ovum.

  (ii) **Oestrogen** endometrial repair and growth.

  (iii) **Oestrogen and progesterone together** prepare endometrium and other parts of the body for pregnancy.

Question 18 What is parturition? Which hormones are involved in induction of parturition?

Sol. Parturition refers to the process of delivery of the mature foetus from the mother's womb, at the end of the pregnancy period. This is induced by a complex neuro-endocrine mechanism. Oxytocin hormone from maternal pituitary stimulates strong uterine contractions that lead to expulsion of the baby from the uterus.

Question 19 In our society the women are often blamed for giving birth to daughters. Can you explain why this is not correct?

Sol. Blaming women for giving birth to girls is scientifically wrong because sex of the baby is determined by father, not by the mother. Women are homogametic, *i.e.* they produce only one type of egg (carrying X chromosome) while males are heterogametic, *i.e.* they produce two types of sperm (carrying X or Y chromosomes)

If the sperm having X-chromosome fertilises the ovum (X), the resulting zygote (XX) will become a female.

If the sperm having Y-chromosome fertilises the ovum (X), the resulting zygote (XY) will become a male.

Question 20 How many eggs are released by a human ovary in a month? How many eggs do you think would have been released if the mother gave birth to identical twins? Would your answer change if the twins born were fraternal?

Sol. Only one egg is released by human ovary in a month.

In case of identical twins, one egg was released which after fertilisation with one sperm, makes a diploid zygote cell. This first cell splits in two embryos and each starts to develop as a separate individual.

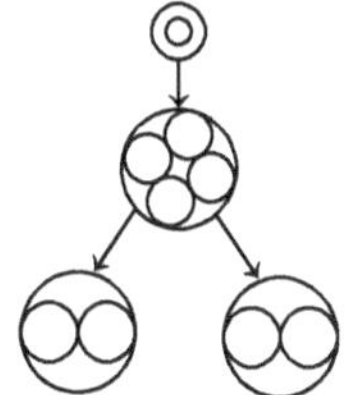

Eggs released with ovary

Since, the origin was a single zygote, both have same genetic constitution and physical appearance.

In case of fraternal (non-identical) twins, two eggs were released, got fertilised by two sperms to make two zygotes that will develop independently.

They develop from two different zygotes with different genetic constitution so, they have different physical appearance.

Question 21 How many eggs do you think were released by the ovary of a female dog which gave birth to six puppies?

Sol. If a female dog gave birth to six puppies, the number of eggs released would be six as dogs are poly-ovulatory species. In such species, more than one ovum is released from ovary at the time of ovulation.

DIKSHA APP Questions

☐ Multiple Choice Questions

Q.1 What is received by Bidder's canal?

(a) Eggs

(b) Sperms

(c) Ammonia

(d) Oxygenated Blood

Sol. (b) Sperms are received by Bidder's canal. Bidder's canal is a structure in the kidneys of male amphibians that transports sperm from the testes to the ureter or cloaca. It is a part of reproductive system.

Q.2 Wolffian duct is also known as

(a) ejaculatory duct

(b) major Sublingual duct

(c) cystic duct

(d) mesonephric duct

Sol. (d) Wolffian duct is also known as mesonephric duct because it originates from the mesonephros, an embryonic kidney structure.

Q.3 Cryptorchidism is a condition which represents

(a) one of both testes are not developed

(b) one or both testes fail to descend into the scrotum

(c) one or both testes are not formed totally

(d) one or both testes are over developed

Sol. (b) Cryptorchidism is a condition in which one or both testes fail to descend into the scrotum during fetal development or shortly after birth.

Q.4 Seminal plasma, the fluid part of semen is formed by

(a) seminal vesicle and bulbourethral gland.

(b) bulbourethral gland and prostate.

(c) prostate and seminal vesicle.

(d) seminal vesicles, prostate and bulbourethral gland.

Sol. (d) Seminal plasma, the fluid part of semen, is formed by secretions from the seminal vesicles, prostate gland, and bulbourethral glands.

Q.5 The hormone that is released from the testes is named as

(a) progesterone

(b) vasopressin

(c) testosterone

(d) spermatosterone

Sol. (a) The hormone released from the testes is called testosterone.

Q.6 Spermiation is the process of the release of sperms from

(a) seminiferous Tubules   (b) vas deferens

(c) epididymis   (d) prostate gland

Sol. (a) Spermiation is the process of releasing sperm from the Sertoli cells into the lumen of the seminiferous tubules.

Q.7 The human sperm locomote through

(a) flagella   (b) cilia   (c) neutrophils   (d) villi

Sol. (a) Human sperm locomote through the female reproductive tract using their flagella, which provides the motility necessary for movement toward the egg.

Q.8 How many autosomes does a human primary spermatocyte have?

(a) 48   (b) 44   (c) 45   (d) 46

Sol. (b) A human primary spermatocyte is a diploid cell, meaning it has 46 chromosomes in total (23 pairs). Since 2 of these chromosomes are sex chromosomes (XY in males), the remaining 44 chromosomes are autosomes.

Q.9 There is no cell division involved in

(a) spermatogenesis   (b) oogenesis

(c) embryogenesis   (d) spermiogenesis

Sol. (d) Spermiogenesis is the process in which spermatids mature into sperm cells. This process involves the transformation of spermatids into functional sperm, but there is no cell division involved, as the spermatids are already haploid.

Q.10 The lytic enzyme released by the sperm is named as

(a) hyaluronidase (b) trypsin   (c) helicase   (d) ligase

Sol. (a) Hyaluronidase is an enzyme released by sperm that helps break down hyaluronic acid in the female reproductive tract, facilitating the sperm's penetration through the egg's protective layers during fertilisation.

Q.11 Which of the following organelle helps the sperm to penetrate the ovum?

(a) Acrosome   (b) Zona Pellucida

(c) Megalis   (d) Ampulla

Sol. (a) The acrosome is the organelle in the sperm that helps it penetrate the ovum. It is located at the tip of the sperm's head and contains enzymes, such as hyaluronidase, that break down the protective layers surrounding the egg, allowing sperm to fertilise the ovum.

Q.12 After the release of the secondary oocyte, the Graafian follicle develops into

(a) corpus callosum (b) corpus albicans
(c) corpus luteum (d) primary follicle

Sol. (c) After the release of the secondary oocyte, the Graafian follicle develops into the corpus luteum. The corpus luteum secretes hormones, primarily progesterone, to maintain the uterine lining for potential pregnancy.

Q.13 Proliferative phase of menstrual cycle is also called

(a) follicular phase (b) luteal phase
(c) secretory phase (d) ovulatory phase

Sol. (a) The proliferative phase of the menstrual cycle is also known as the follicular phase. During this phase, the endometrium (uterine lining) thickens in response to rising levels of oestrogen, and follicles in the ovaries mature.

Q.14 Where does the ovum receive the sperm?

(a) Animal pole (b) Vegetal pole
(c) Zona pellucida (d) Flagellum

Sol. (a) The ovum receives sperm at the animal pole of the egg. The animal pole is the region of the egg where the sperm typically enters, while the vegetal pole is the opposite side, where the yolk is concentrated.

Q.15 Which of the following hormones prepares the uterus for implantation?

(a) Progesterone (b) FSH
(c) Oestrogen (d) LH

Sol. (a) Progesterone is secreted by the corpus luteum after ovulation and helps to thicken the endometrium (uterine lining), making it suitable for the implantation of a fertilised egg.

Q.16 The outermost layer of a blastocyst is called

(a) ectoderm (b) mesoderm
(c) endoderm (d) trophoblast

Sol. (d) The trophoblast plays a key role in implantation by attaching the blastocyst to the uterine wall and eventually developing into the placenta.

☐ Long Answer Type

Q.1 Explain the difference between the meiotic division of oogenesis and spermatogenesis in detail.

Sol. Oogenesis and spermatogenesis both involve meiotic divisions to produce gametes, but differ in outcomes. In oogenesis, one functional egg is produced from each precursor cell, with three polar bodies that degenerate. Meiosis is arrested in prophase I until puberty and completes only if fertilization occurs. In spermatogenesis, four sperm cells are produced from each precursor cell through two symmetrical meiotic divisions. Thus, oogenesis produces one egg, while spermatogenesis produces four sperm.

Q.2 Explain the role of pituitary gonadotropins during the follicular and ovulatory phases of the menstrual cyde. Describe the shifts in steroidal secretions.

Sol. In the follicular phase (Days 1-14), FSH stimulates the growth of ovarian follicles and the production of estrogen. Estrogen thickens the endometrial lining. LH remains low initially but rises as follicles mature.

In the ovulatory phase (around Day 14), the peak in estrogen levels triggers a LH surge, which causes ovulation (release of the egg). FSH also rises slightly. Estrogen peaks just before ovulation, and progesterone, remains low.

After ovulation, the corpus luteum forms and secretes progesterone, preparing the uterus for a potential pregnancy.

Reproductive Health

Important Points

01 **Reproductive Health** means a complete well being in all aspects of reproduction. This includes not only normal structure and function of reproductive organs, but also healthy emotional, behavioural and social outlook towards sex and reproduction.

02 **Poor Reproductive Health** is frequently associated with disease, abuse, exploitation, unwanted pregnancy and death.

03 **Strategies to Improve Reproductive Health**
   (i) Family planning programmes were initiated by government of India in 1951.
   (ii) 'Reproductive and Child Health Care (RCH) programmes' were launched to created awareness among people about various reproduction related aspects.
   (iii) Counseling about safe and responsible sex to clear misconceptions and myths.
   (iv) Prevention of sex abuse and sex related crimes.

04 **Amniocentesis** It is a test done during pregnancy to detect birth defects and genetic problems in the developing baby.

However, it has been more commonly used as fetal sex determination test, which led to large scale female foeticide.

05 Improved health facilities and better living conditions have promoted the community health, but has also contributed to explosive growth of population. This can lead to an absolute scarcity of even the basic requirements, *i.e.* food, shelter and clothing.

06 To address overpopulation, measures like promoting smaller families through contraceptives, raising the marriageable age and offering incentives for small families are encouraged.

07 **An Ideal Contraceptive** should be user friendly, effective and non-intefering with sexual drive or act of the user.

08 A variety of contraceptive methods are discussed below.

(i) **Natural Methods of Birth Control** work on the principle of avoiding chances of ovum and sperms meeting. It can be accomplished by following means :

- **Periodic abstinence** A method in which the couples avoid or abstain from intercourse during the woman's fertile period.
- **Withdrawal** or **coitus interruptus** is a method in which the male partner withdraws his penis from the vagina just before ejaculation, to avoid release of sperm inside.
- **Lactational amenorrhea** (absence of menstruation during lactation) This method is based on the fact that ovulation does not occur during the period of intense lactation following childbirth thus, preventing chances of pregnancy.

(ii) **Use of Physical Barriers to Avoid Meeting of Sperm and Ovum**

- **Condoms** are barriers made of thin, rubber/ latex sheath that are worn over the penis in males or used to cover the vagina and cervix in females, just before intercourse so that the ejaculated semen would not enter into the female reproductive tract.
- **Diaphragms, cervical caps** and **vaults** are also barriers made of rubber that are inserted into the female reproductive tract to cover cervix during coitus. They are reusable.
- **Spermicidal creams, jellies** and **foams** are also used along with the barriers to increase their efficiency.

(iii) **Intra Uterine Devices** (IUDs) are effective and popular method of contraception. These devices have to be inserted by medical practitioners in the uterus through vagina.

Intra Uterine Devices are presently available as

(a) Non-medicated IUDs (*e.g.*, Lippes loop).

(b) Copper releasing IUDs (*e.g.*, Cu-T, Cu-7, Multiload 375).

(c) Hormone releasing IUDs (*e.g.*, Progestasert, LNG-20).

(iv) **Oral contraceptives** This involves uptake of hormonal preparation of either progestogens or progestogen estrogen combinations in the form of pills by female.

Saheli is the new oral contraceptive for the females which contains a non-steroidal preparation. It is a 'once a week' pill with fewer side effects and high contraceptive value.

(v) **Hormonal Injections/Implants** Progestogens can also used by females as injections and implants under the skin to inhibit ovulation. Injectables are given in every 1-3 months.

(vi) **Surgical Methods**, also called **sterilisation**, are generally advised for the male/female partner as a terminal method to prevent any more pregnancies. Surgical intervention blocks gamete transport and thereby prevent conception.

Sterilisation procedure in the male is called 'vasectomy' and that in the female, 'tubectomy'.

09 **Medical Termination of Pregnancy** (MTP) It is intentional or voluntary termination of pregnancy before full term

(i) Government of India legalized MTP in 1971 with some strict conditions to avoid its misuse, as such female foeticide.

(ii) MTPs are considered relatively safe during the first trimester (up to 12 weeks) of pregnancy.

10 **Sexually Transmitted Diseases** (STDs) are diseases or infections which are transmitted through sexual intercourse.

Gonorrhoea, syphilis, genital herpes, chlamydiasis, genital warts, trichomoniasis, hepatitis-B and HIV leading to AIDS are some of the common STDs or RTIs (Reproductive tract infections).

11 **Infertility** It is defined as an inablity to produce children in spite of unprotected sexual co-habitation. The reasons could be congenital, diseases, drugs, immunological, physical or even psychological.

12 **Assisted reproductive technologies (ART) are-medical procedures used to help couples with infertility.**

- Methods like *In vitro* fertilisation (IVF) involve combining eggs and sperm outside the body to create embryos, which are then transferred to the uterus or fallopian tube (ZIFT, IUT)for further development.
- Gamete intra-fallopian transfer (GIFT)allows eggs from a donor to be placed in the fallopian tube of another woman, while intracytoplasmic sperm injection (ICSI) directly injects a sperm into an egg to form an embryo.
- Artificial insemination (AI),and intra-uterine insemination (IUI) involve the introduction of sperm into the female reproductive system to aid fertilisation.

Exercises

Question 1 What do you think is the significance of reproductive health in a society?

Sol. Significance of reproductive health in a society are
  (i) control over the transmission of STDs.
  (ii) reduction in death due to reproduction related diseases like–AIDS and cancer of reproductive tract.
  (iii) control in population explosion.
  (iv) additionally, reproductive health of men and women affects the health of the next generation.
  (v) Obtaining treatment for reproductive disorders at the earliest.

Question 2 Suggest the aspects of reproductive health which need to be given special attention in the present scenario.

Sol. The aspects of reproductive health which need to be given special attention in the present scenario are as follows.
  (i) Educating people (starting from age group above 12 years) about reproductive system, processes and practices and importance of safe and responsible sex.
  (ii) Educating people about harmful sexual practices, unwanted pregnancy, unsafe abortion and reproductive tract infections (STDs).
  (iii) Establishing proper systems of education, counselling, prevention, detection and management of reproduction related problems.
  (iv) Creating awareness of problems due to uncontrolled population growth, social evils like sexual abuse, etc.
  (v) More health clinic with infrastructural facilities and professional espects.

Question 3 Is sex education necessary in schools? Why?

Sol. Yes, sex education in schools is absolutely necessary because
  (i) It would provide the right information to the young minds at about various aspects of reproductive health such as reproductive organs, puberty, safe sexual practices and sexually transmitted diseases.
  (ii) It would provide right information to avoid myths and misconceptions about sex-related queries.

Question 4 Do you think that reproductive health in our country has improved in the past 50 years? If yes, mention some such areas of improvement.

Sol.   Reproductive health has improved in India in the past 50 years in terms of
   (i)   reduced maternal and infant mortality rates.
   (ii) early detection and cure of STDs.
   (iii) assistance to infertile couples.
   (iv) availability of a variety of methods for family planning.
   (v)   availability of maternal and child health care programs.
   (vi) introduction of sex education in schools.

Question 5 What are the suggested reasons for population explosion?

Sol.   The reasons for population explosion are as follows.
   (i)   Ignorance and complete lack of awareness about the ill effects of increasing population especially in rural regions.
   (ii) Increased health facilities along with better living conditions.
   (iii) Decline in death rate.
   (iv) Decline in maternal and infant mortality rate.
   (v)   Increase in the young, reproductive age population.
   (vi) Lack of education.

Question 6 Is the use of contraceptives justified? Give reasons.

Sol.   Yes, the use of contraceptives is justified because of the following reasons.
   (i)   In the absence of contraceptives, the population growth rate will explode and there will be scarcity of even the basic necessities. Contraceptives help to control the rapid growth of human population.
   (ii) Contraceptives provide an option for planning the family by spacing the pregnancies and avoiding unwanted pregnancies.
   (iii) Contraceptives also guard against STDs to some extent.

Question 7 Removal of gonads cannot be considered as a contraceptive option. Why?

Sol.   Contraception is meant for preventing conceptions and not affecting body functions, including appearance and physiology. Removal of gonads cannot be considered a contraceptive option because it will lead to infertility and unavailability of certain hormones that are required for the normal functioning of the body. Moreover, once removed, gonads can't be replaced and the person will remain infertile for life.

Question 8 Amniocentesis for sex determination is banned in our country. Is this ban necessary? Comment.

Sol. Yes, the ban on amniocentesis is necessary because it is misused to determine the sex of the foetus which in turn to female foeticide. It became so serious that it disturbed the male female ratio that can have a negative impact on society.

Question 9 Suggest some methods to assist infertile couples to have children.

Sol. Infertile couples can have children by following methods.

  (i) *In vitro* **Fertilisation** (IVF) or **test tube baby** programme in this method, ova from the wife/donor (female) and sperms from the husband/donor (male) are induced to form zygote under controlled conditions in the laboratory. The zygote or early embryos is then implanted in the mother.

  (ii) **Gamete Intra Fallopian Transfer** (GIFT) It involes transfer of an ovum, collected from a donor female, into the Fallopian tube of another female who cannot produce one, but can provide suitable environment for fertilisation and further development of foetus.

  (iii) **Intra Cytoplasmic Sperm Injection** (ICSI) It is a specialised procedure to form an embryo in the lab in which a sperm is artificially injected into the ovum, using a microsyringe.

  (iv) **Artificial Insemination** (AI) Infertility due to inability of the male partner to inseminate the female or due to very low sperm counts in the ejaculation, could be corrected by AI.

In this technique, the semen is collected from the husband or a healthy donor and is artificially introduced into the vagina or the uterus (IUI—Intra-Uterine Insemination) of the female.

Question 10 What are the measures one has to take to prevent from contracting STDs?

Sol. Measures to prevent from contracting STDs are as follows.

  (i) Avoid sex with unknown partners/multiple partners.

  (ii) Always use condom during intercourse.

  (iii) In case of doubt, immediately go to a qualified doctor for early detection and get complete treatment if diagnosed with disease.

Question 11 State True/False with explanation.

(a) Abortions could happen spontaneously too.   (True/False)

(b) Infertility is defined as the inability to produce a viable offspring and is always due to abnormalities/defects in the female partner.
(True/False)

(c) Complete lactation could help as a natural method of contraception.   (True/False)

(d) Creating awareness about sex related aspects is an effective method to improve reproductive health of the people.   (True/False)

Sol. (a) True, Due to poor health of mother or poor development of foetus abortion can happen spontaneously.

(b) False, Infertility is defined as the inability to produce viable offspring even after unprotected sexual co-habitation. It is due to abnormalities/ defects in either male or female or both the parents.

(c) Ture, Lactational amenorrhea has been reported to be effective only upto a maximum period of six months following parturition.

(d) True, Creating awareness about sex-related aspects removes the myths and misconception about these problems.

Question 12 Correct the following statements.

(a) Surgical methods of contraception prevent gamete formation.

(b) All sexually transmitted diseases are completely curable.

(c) Oral pills are very popular contraceptives among the rural women.

(d) In ET techniques, embryos are always transferred into the uterus.

Sol. Corrected statements :

(a) Surgical methods of contraception prevent gamete transport and thereby prevent conception.

(b) Only a few sexually transmitted diseases are completely curable if diagnosed early and treated appropriately.

(c) Oral pills are very popular contraceptives among the urban women.

(d) In ET techniques, embryos with 8 blastomeres are transferred into the Fallopian tubes and embryos with more than 8-blastomeres are generally transferred into the uterus.

DIKSHA APP Questions

☐ Multiple Choice Questions

Q.1 Amniocentesis is conducted to

(a) detect any genetic disorder of the foetus
(b) kill the female foetus
(c) abort unwanted pregnancy
(d) detect sex of the baby

Sol. (a) Amniocentesis is a medical procedure, involving collection of amniotic fluid to detect genetic disorders, such as Down syndrome, in the fetus.

Q.2 The injections and implants used by females as contraceptives contain

(a) progesteron and oestrogen   (b) testosterone
(c) corticosteroids   (d) androgens

Sol. (a) The injections and implants used by females as contraceptives typically contain synthetic forms of progesterone and oestrogen, which prevent ovulation and reduce the chances of pregnancy.

Q.3 Which one of the following are IUDs?

(a) Cu-T, Cu7, Multiload 375   (b) LNG-20
(c) STD   (d) Both a and b

Sol. (d) CuT, Cu7 and Multiload 375 are copper releasing IUDs and LNG-20 is a hormone releasing IUD.

Q.4 SAHELI works by

(a) inhibiting ovulation and implantation
(b) once in a week pill
(c) Both a and b
(d) only a

Sol. (c) SAHELI is an once in a week pill that works by inhibiting ovulation and also makes the uterine lining less suitable for the implantation of a fertilised egg.

Q.5 SAHELI is

(a) an oral female contraceptive   (b) a male contraceptive
(c) an IUD   (d) a Mechanical barrier

Sol. (a) SAHELI is a non-hormonal contraceptive pill designed for females.

Q.6 Which of the following are used as male contraception?

a. Vasectomy   b. Tubectomy   c. Condoms   d. MTP.

(a) a and c   (b) a and b   (c) b and c   (d) None

Sol. (a) Vasectomy is a surgical male contraception method that blocks sperm flow, while condoms are a non-surgical barrier method preventing sperm from reaching the female reproductive tract.

Q.7 The permanent sterilisation of females is called

(a) vasectomy   (b) tubectomy   (c) MTP   (d) STD

Sol. (b) Tubectomy is the permanent sterilisation of females, where the fallopian tubes are surgically removed or sealed to prevent pregnancy.

Q.8 Some of the following are sexually transmitted diseases. Identify the pair shown in the options.

a. gonorrhea   b. syphills   c. taeniasis   d. paralysis

(a) a and b   (b) b and c

(c) c and d   (d) All of these

Sol. (a) Gonorrhea and syphilis are sexually transmitted diseases (STDs) caused by bacteria.

□ Very Short Answer Type

Q.1 What are the 4 major objectives of RCH?

Sol. Aim of reproductive and child health care (RCH) programme is to improve reproductive health of the society. The four major objectives undertaken by this programme are as follows-

   I. Aware people about various reproduction related aspects.

   II. Provide facilities and support for making a society reproductively healthy.

   III. Aware people for prenatal and postnatal care of mother and child.

   IV. Educate couples about child birth.

Q.2 What is lactational amenorrhea? Explain how it is advantageous to couples?

Sol. Lactational amenorrhea is the absence of menstruation in lactating mothers. It is a period of temporary infertility or postpartum infertility. It is advantageous to couples because, therefore, as long as the mother breast-feeds the child fully, chances of conception are almost nil. However, this method has been reported to be effective only upto a maximum period of six months following parturition. As no medicines or devices are used in these methods, side effects are almost nil.

Q.3 What is STD? Write any three such diseases caused to human beings.

Sol. Diseases which are transmitted through sexual intercourse are collectively called sexually transmitted diseases (STD).

e.g.,- hepatitis- B, genital herpes, HIV leading to AIDS are some of the common STD's.

☐ Long Answer Type

Q.1 Explain what are *in-vitro, in-vivo* and AI fertilisation techniques used in ART?

Sol. The couples could be assisted to have children through certain special techniques commonly known as assisted reproductive technologies (ART)

The different techniques used in ART are discussed below

1. *In Vitro* **Fertilisation (IVF)** This method involves fertilising eggs outside the body under controlled laboratory conditions, similar to the natural process. The fertilised eggs (zygotes) or early embryos are then transferred to the fallopian tube (ZIFT) or uterus (IUT) for further development.

2. *In Vivo* **Fertilisation** In this approach, fertilisation occurs naturally within the female's body, and the resulting embryos are then transferred to the fallopian tube or uterus to assist in conception.

3. **Artificial Insemination (AI)** In this method, semen collected from the husband or a donor is artificially introduced into the female's vagina or uterus (IUI), which help to increase the chances of fertilisation.

Principles of Inheritance and Variation

CHAPTER 04

Important Points

01 Important Key Terms

(i) **Genetics** is the branch of science that deals with the study of genes, heredity and variation in organisms and also the application of principles of inheritance.

(ii) **Inheritance** is the process of transfer of characters or traits from one generation to the next.

(iii) Parents pass on information encoded in **genes**, packed as **chromosomes**, to their progeny because of which the progeny resemble the parents in morphological and physiological features.

(iv) **A truebreeding** line, shows 'stable trait inheritance and expression', for several generations, as it has undergone continuous self-pollination.

(v) **Progeny** refers to the offsprings or next generation. First filial generation is termed as F_1 generation, second as F_2 and so on.

(vi) **Trait/character** refers to the expression of genes in the form of visible physical properties, *e.g.*, colour of flower, height of plant, shape of leaf, etc.

(vii) **Gene** is a unit of inheritance, a sequence of DNA that codes for a specific polypeptide.

(viii) **Alleles** are slightly different forms of the same gene, *e.g.*, a gene codes for the colour of eyes. One of its form codes for brown and another codes for blue colour.

(ix) **Genotype** refers to the genetic constitution of an individual.

(x) **Phenotype** refers to observable traits or characters that result from expression of genes.

(xi) **Homozygous** condition means having a pair of identical alleles (forms of gene) at a gene location (locus) on a pair of homologous chromosomes.

(xii) **Heterozygous** condition means having a pair of non-identical alleles, at a gene locus on a pair of homologous chromosomes.

(xiii) **Dominant** allele expresses itself even in the presence of another non-identical allele.

(xiv) **Recessive** allele does not expresses itself in the presence of another non-identical allele. It expresses only in the presence of another identical allele or when no other allele is present.

(xv) **Hybrid** is an organism produced from crossbreeding of two different varieties, species or genetic traits.

(xvi) **Monohybrid** is a hybrid for a single gene or a single trait.

(xvii) **Dihybrid** is a hybrid for two genes or two traits.

(xviii) **Punnett square** is a graphical representation that is used to calculate the probability of all possible genotypes of offspring in a genetic cross.

(xix) **Back cross** The cross of the hybrids of F_1-generation with either of its parents.

(xx) **Test cross** is an experiment used to determine the genotype of an organism by crossing F_1 hybrid with the recessive parent.

(xxi) **Linkage** refers to the physical association of genes on a chromosome.

(xxii) **Recombination** refers to the generation of new combination of genes.

(xxiii) **Sex chromosomes** are the chromosomes in sexually reproducing species that determine the gender of the individual.

(xxiv) **Autosomes** are chromosomes that are not involved in determining the sex of an individual and are same in both males and females of a species.

(xxv) **Heterogamety** occurs when two different types of gametes are produced by an individual. Human males produce two types of gametes, one type with X-chromosome and another with Y-chromosome.

(xxvi) **Homogamety** occurs when only one type of gametes are produced by an individual. Human females produce gametes with X-chromosome only.

(xxvii) **Polygenic inheritance** involves multiple genes contributing to a single trait, resulting in a continuous range of phenotypes.

(xxviii) **Pleiotropy** occurs when one gene influences multiple, seemingly unrelated traits or characters.

(xxix) **Mutation** a change in DNA sequence. It could be a single xbase pair change or bigger.

(xxx) **Pedigree** is a chart that shows genetic connections among individuals in a line of ancestors; a lineage or a family tree.

(xxxi) **Pedigree Analysis** is a genetic tool used to study the inheritance patterns of traits within a family.

(xxxii) **Chromosomal disorders** occur by the alteration or mutation in a gene resulting in abnormal expression of a trait, function of an enzyme or shape of a cell.

02 Mendel and his Experiments on Patterns of Inheritance Mendel conducted artificial pollination/cross pollination experiments using several true-breeding lines in pea plant.

Mendel selected 14 true-breeding pea plant varieties and made pairs. The pairs were similar except for one contrasting trait, *e.g.,* smooth or wrinkled seeds, yellow or green seeds, smooth or inflated pods, green or yellow pods, tall or dwarf plants, axial or terminal flower and yellow or white flowers. In a pair one being the dominant trait (tall) and another being the recessive trait (dwarf).

03 Mendel's Observations Observations laid the foundation for modern genetics. By studying pea plants Mendel observed that traits are inherited in predictable patterns.

04 Mendel's Laws of Inheritance Mendel proposed three laws of inheritance based on his experiments with pea plants. These laws are as follows.

(i) **Law of dominance**

(a) Characters are controlled by the discrete units called **factors**.

(b) Factors occur in pairs.

(c) In a dissimilar pair of factors, one member dominates and expresses as trait (dominant), while the other remain unexpressed (recessive).

The law of dominance explains the expression of only one of the parental characters in a monohybrid cross in the F_1-generation and the expression of both in the F_2-generations. It also explains the proportion of 3 : 1 obtained at the F_2-generations.

(ii) **Law of segregation**

    (a) This law is based on the fact that the alleles do not show any blending and that both the characters are recovered as such in the F_2-generation though one of these is not seen at the F_1-stage.

    (b) Diploid cells have pairs of alleles on homologous chromosomes (pair = one chromosome from egg or mother and one from sperm or father). During meiosis, one pair of alleles segregate and end up in different gametes.

    (c) A homozygous parent produces all the gametes that are similar, while a heterozygous one produces two kinds of gametes each having one allele from the pair.

(iii) **Law of independent assortment**

    (a) The law states that when two pairs of traits are combined in a hybrid, segregation of one pair of characteris independent of the other pair of character.

    (b) The inheritance of one character does not effect the inheritance of other.

05 **True Dominance** If one allele of a pair completely masks the expression of the other allele in a heterozygous condition, it called true dominance.

06 **Incomplete Dominance** If one allele of a pair does not completely dominate the other in a heterozygous condition, it is called **incomplete dominance**. In this case, the heterozygous phenotype is a blend or intermediate between two homozygous phenotype.

e.g. A plant (snapdragon) true breeding for red flower, if crossed with plant true breeding for white flower, the hybrids of next generation show pink flowers.

07 **Co-dominance** Sometimes, both the alleles dominate in a heterozygous condition, it is called co-dominance. In this case, both the alleles express simultaneous and F_1-generation displays both parents. An example is different types of red blood cells that determine ABO blood grouping in human beings.

The ABO blood group is controlled by the gene I.

The gene I has three alleles I^A, I^B and i.

The alleles I^A and I^B produce antigen A and antigen B respectively on the surface of RBC while allele (i) doesn't produce any antigen.

I^A and I^B are dominant over i.

When I^A and i are present, it shows blood group A.

When I^B and i are present, it shows blood group B.

When I^A and I^B are together, both express their antigens due to co-dominance, Hence blood group AB is the example of co-dominance.

08 Chromosomal Theory of Inheritance The theory states that genes are located on chromosomes and that the inheritance of trait is governed by the segregation and independent assortment of chromosomes during meiosis. This theory connects Mendelian genetics with behavior of chromosomes.

09 Sex determination The method by which the distinction between male and female is established in a species. Sex determination can be chromosomal, with XX/XY in mammals and ZZ/ZW in birds, or genic, where specific gene determine sex. In haplodiploidy, sex is determined by the number of chromosome sets, with haploid males and diploid female in honeybees.

10 Mendelian or Chromosomal Disorders

(i) **Haemophilia** It is a sex-linked recessive genetic disorder inherited from a mother who is a carrier of abnormal gene present on the X-chromosome. It is expressed only in males as they do not have another allele on their Y-chromosome to mask the effect of the defective gene. In this disease, a single protein that is a part of the cascade of proteins involved in the clotting of blood is affected. If an individual once wounded, the bleeding does not stop.

(ii) **Colour blindness** it is a sex-linked recessive disorders due to defect in either red or green cone of eye resulting in failure to discriminate between red and green colour.

(iii) **Sickle cell anaemia** It is an autosome-linked recessive trait that can be transmitted from heterozygous carrier parents to the offspring. The defect results from the substitution of glutamic acid (Glu) by valine (Val) at the sixth position of the beta globin chain of the haemoglobin molecule.

The mutant haemoglobin molecule undergoes polymerisation under low oxygen tension causing the change in the shape of the RBC from biconcave disc to elongated sickle-like structure.

(iv) **Phenylketonuria** This inborn error of metabolism is also inherited as the autosomal recessive trait. Individual lacks an enzyme that converts the amino acid phenylalanine into tyrosine. As a result, phenylalanine is accumulated and converted into phenyl pyruvic acid and other derivatives. Accumulation of these products in brain results in mental retardation. These are also excreted through the urine because of its poor absorption by kidney.

(v) **Thalassemia** It is an autosomal recessive blood disease which occurs due to either mutation or deletion of one or more gene, resulting in reduced rate of synthesis of one of the globin chain that make up haemoglobin. This causes the formation of abnormal haemoglobin molecules, resulting into anaemia.

11 Chromosomal Disorders The chromosomal disorders are caused due to the absence or excess or abnormal arrangement of one or more chromosomes. Failure of segregation of chromatids during cell division cycle results in the gain or loss of a chromosome(s), called **aneuploidy**. Failure of cytokinesis after telophase stage of cell division results in a increase in a whole set of chromosome, this phenomenon is known as polyploidy.

(i) **Down's syndrome** caused by an additional copy of the chromosome number 21 (trisomy of 21). The affected individual is short statured with small round head, furrowed tongue and partially open mouth. Physical, psychomotor and mental development is retarded.

(ii) **Klinefelter's syndrome** is caused due to the presence of an additional copy of X-chromosome resulting into a karyotype of 47, XXY. Such an individual has overall masculine development, but a few feminine features as well, *e.g.* development of breast (gynaecomastia). Affected individuals are sterile.

(iii) **Turner's syndrome** is caused due to the absence of one of the X-chromosomes, *i.e.* 45 with XO. Such females have webbed neck, shield-shaped thorax, rudimentary ovaries, absence of other secondary sexual characters.

Exercises

Question 1 Mention the advantages of selecting pea plant for experiment by Mendel.

Sol.   Advantages of selecting pea plant are as follows

   (i) Pea plant showed visible contrasting characters, *e.g.,* tall/dwarf plants, round/wrinkled seeds, green/yellow pods, etc. It was easy to track the passing on of these characters in the progeny.

  (ii) The pea flower is bisexual and therefore undergoes self-pollination easily. Thus, pea plant produce offspring with same traits generation after generation.

 (iii) Cross-pollination can be easily achieved.

 (iv) Many seeds are produced in one generation.

  (v) Pea plant has short life cycle which allowed to observe multiple generations in a short period.

 (vi) It is easy to grow.

Question 2 Differentiate between the following
   (i) Dominance and Recessive
  (ii) Homozygous and Heterozygous
 (iii) Monohybrid and Dihybrid

Sol.   (i) **Dominant** A character that is expressed in both homozygous and heterozygous conditions (even in the presence of another different allele).

   Recessive   A character that expresses itself only in homozygous condition (both alleles of the same character), but remains unexpressed in heterozygous condition.

  (ii) **Homozygous** It is a condition, where an individual has two identical alleles for a particular gene.

   Heterozygous It is a condition, where an individual has two different types of alleles for a gene.

 (iii) **Monohybrid** if an individual is heterozygous for only one trait, *e.g.* only eye colour.

   Dihybrid if an individual is heterozygous for two traits, *e.g.* eye colour and shape of the eye or eye colour and hair colour.

Question 3 A diploid organism is heterozygous for four loci, how many types of gametes can be produced?

Sol. For a diploid organism that is heterozygous for 4 loci, the number of types of gametes that can be produced is determined by the formula.

No of gametes = 2^n

When n is the number of heterozygous loci

Since the organism is heterozygous for 4 loci, the number of types of gametes that can be produced is

$$2^4 = 16$$

Thus, 16 types of gametes can be produced.

Question 4 Explain the law of dominance using a monohybrid cross.

Sol. When a cross is performed between two individuals taking a single contrasting character at a time, it is called a monohybrid cross. According to the law of dominance, when two different allelomorphic forms of a gene are present in an organism, only one expresses itself in F_1 - generation which is called dominant gene, while the other which does not show its effect and remains masked is called recessive gene. The character 'height' has two alleles 'T' and 't'.

'T' is for tallness, whereas 't' is for dwarfness. When a pure tall (TT) pea plant is crossed with a pure dwarf (tt) plant in the F_1- generation, hybrid 'Tt' is obtained which is tall due to the presence of allele 'T'. This shows that tallness is dominant over dwarfness. Diagrammatically it can be explained as.

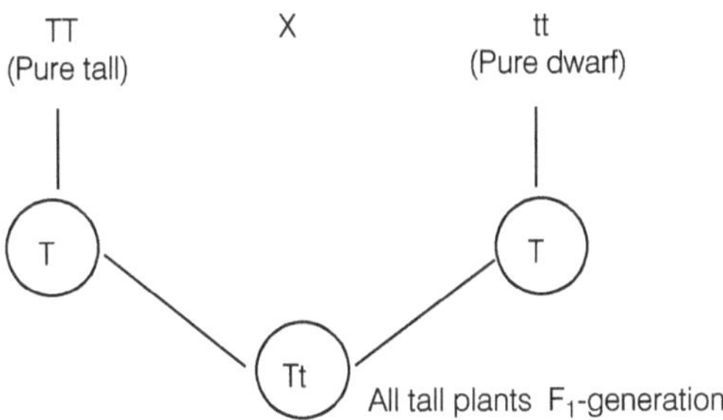

Question 5 Define and design a test-cross.

Sol. A test cross is a genetic cross between an individual with unknown dominant genotype and a homozygous recessive individual. This helps to determine whether the unknown genotype is homozygous dominant or heterozygous dominant.

Design of a test-cross

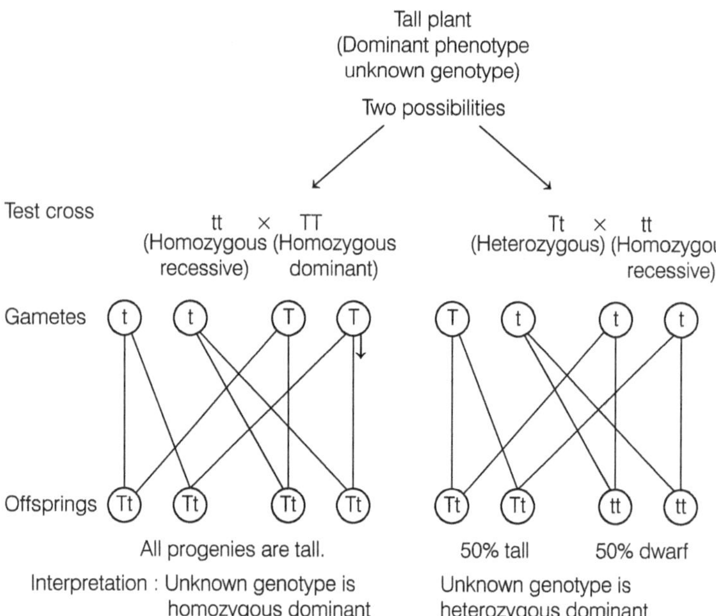

Question 6 Using a Punnett square, workout the distribution of phenotypic features in the first filial generation after a cross between a homozygous female and a heterozygous male for a single locus.

Sol. Parent generation (genotype)   Homozygous female Heterozygous male

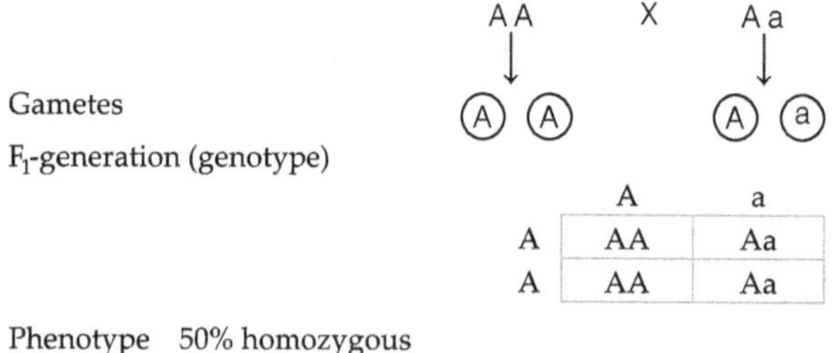

Phenotype   50% homozygous

50% heterozygous F_1 ratio = 1 : 1.

Question 7 When a cross is made between tall plant with yellow seeds (TtYy) and tall plant with green seed (Ttyy), what proportions of phenotype in the offspring could be expected to be

   (a) tall and green   (b) dwarf and green

Sol.

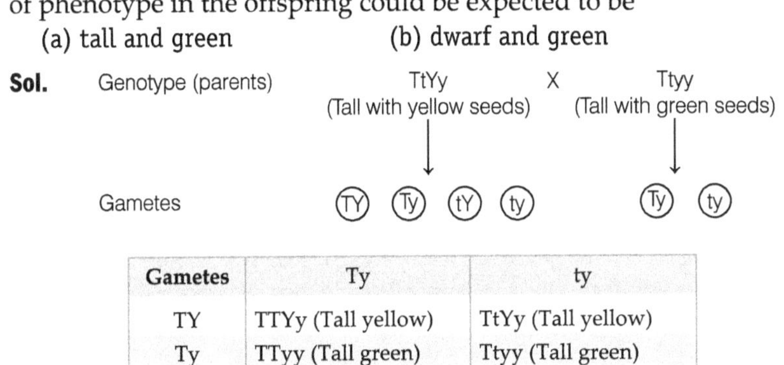

Gametes	Ty	ty
TY	TTYy (Tall yellow)	TtYy (Tall yellow)
Ty	TTyy (Tall green)	Ttyy (Tall green)
tY	TtYy (Tall yellow)	ttYy (Dwarf yellow)
ty	Ttyy (Tall green)	ttyy (Dwarf green)

Proportion of tall and green is 3/8

Proportion of dwarf and green = 1/8

Question 8 Two heterozygous parents are crossed. If the two loci are linked, what would be the distribution of phenotypic features in F_1-generation for a dihybrid cross?

Sol. In a dihybrid cross with linked loci, most F_1 offspring will display the parental phenotypes due to the genes being inherited together. Recombinant phenotype will appear less frequently, depending on the distance between linked genes.

Question 9 Briefly mention the contribution of TH Morgan in genetics.

Sol. TH Morgan's contribution in genetics are as follows.

  (i) Morgan contributed to the understanding of sex-linked traits.

  (ii) He carried out several experiments on fruit flies and his dihybrid crosses revealed that genes for some traits did not segregate independently and the F_2 ratio was a lot different from $9 : 3 : 3 : 1$ (expected when two genes show independent assortment.)

  (iii) He inferred that when two genes were situated on the same chromosome, the proportions of parental gene combinations were significantly higher than the non-parental type.

  (iv) He established the principle of linkage, crossing over and sex-linked inheritance through his work on fruit flies.

  (v) He established the technique of chromosome mapping.

  (vi) He observed and worked on mutation.

Question 10 What is pedigree analysis? Suggest how such an analysis can be useful?

Sol. A pedigree is a chart that shows genetic relationships and inheritance pattern among individuals within the same lineage. An analysis of inheritance of a trait over several generations of a family is called pedigree analysis.

Uses

(i) It is used to track inheritance of a specific trait.

(ii) It is used to know the possibility of expressive or recessive allele which may cause genetic disorder, *e.g.* colour blindness.

(iii) It predicts the harmful effects of marriage between close relatives.

(iv) It helps in genetic counselling to avoid disorders in children.

(v) It is useful in medical research.

Question 11 How is sex determined in human beings?

Sol. In humans, sex is determined by two chromosomes, X and Y, called sex chromosomes. The females have a pair of X-chromosomes (homogametic) and the males have XY (heterogametic) composition. Both male and female have same number of chromosomes.

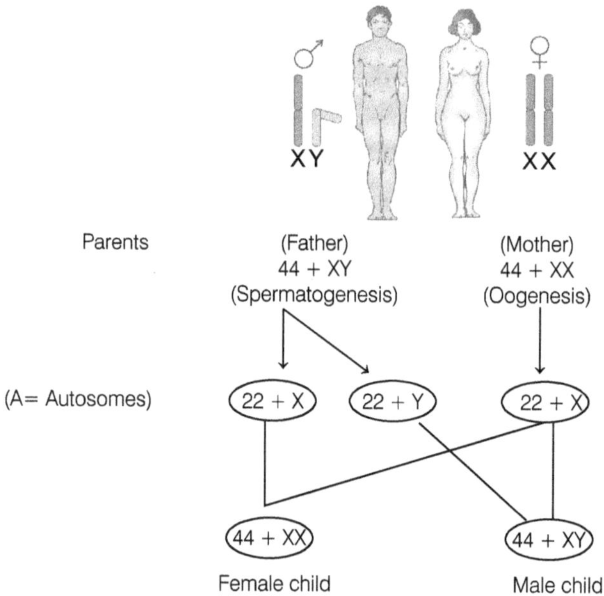

Question 12 A child has blood group O. If the father has blood group A and mother blood group B, work out the genotypes of the parents and the possible genotypes of the other offsprings.

Sol. The child with blood group 'O' will have homozygous recessive alleles (ii). Therefore, both the parents should be heterozygous, *i.e.* the genotype of father will be $I^A i$ and of mother will be $I^B i$.

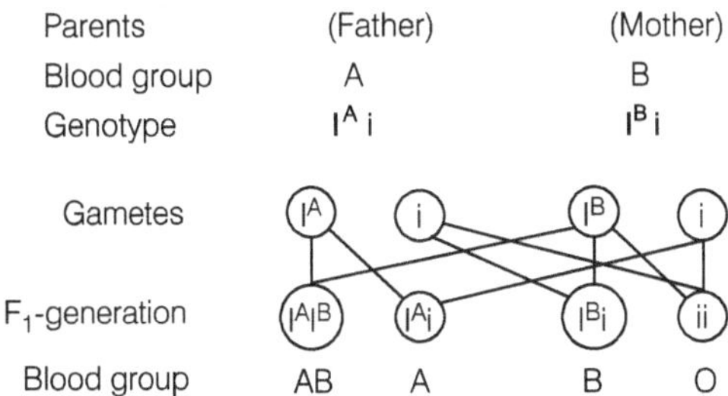

The possible blood groups of other offspring will be AB, A, B and O.

Question 13 Explain the following terms with example

(a) Co-dominance

(b) Incomplete dominance

Sol. (a) **Co-dominance** The condition in which both the alleles of a genotype are fully expressed, resulting in a phenotype that display both traits simultaneously. For example, in human blood type the AB blood group demonstrate co-dominance.

(b) **Incomplete dominance** The condition in which neither allele in a genotype is completely dominant over the other leading to an intermediate phenotype in heterozygous state. For example, in snapdragon, crossing a red flowered plant (RR) with a white flowered plants produces pink-flowered plant (Rr).

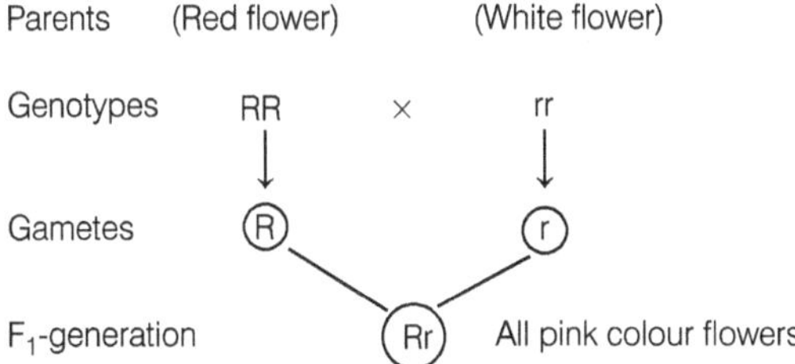

Question 14 What is point mutation? Give an example.

Sol. Point mutation is a change in single base pair of DNA molecule.

Example, Sickle cell anaemia is an autosome linked recessive trait that can be transmitted to the offspring from heterozygous carrier parents.

The defect is caused by the substitution of glutamic acid (Glu) by valine (Val) at the sixth position of the beta globin chain of the haemoglobin molecule.

The substitution of amino acid in the globin protein occurs due to the single base substitution at the sixth codon of the beta globin gene from GAG to GUG. The mutant haemoglobin molecule undergoes polymerisation under low oxygen tension causing the change in the shape of the RBC from biconcave disc to elongated sickle like structure.

Question 15 Who had proposed the chromosomal theory of the inheritance?

Sol. Sutton and Boveri proposed the chromosomal theory of inheritance in 1902.

Question 16 Mention any two autosomal genetic disorders with their symptoms.

Sol. **Phenylketonuria** This inborn error of metabolism is also inherited as the autosomal recessive trait. The affected individual lacks an enzyme that converts the amino acid phenylalanine into tyrosine. As a result, this phenylalanine is accumulated and converted into phenyl pyruvic acid and other derivatives. Accumulation of these in brain results in mental retardation.

Sickle cell anaemia This is an autosome linked recessive trait that can be transmitted from parents to the offspring when both the partners are carrier for the gene (heterozygous). The symptoms of the disease include chronic anaemia, severe pain episodes, frequent infections etc.

DIKSHA APP *Questions*

☐ Multiple Choice Questions

Q.1 Who is called the 'Father of Genetics'?

(a) Johannsen   (b) Gregor Mendel (c) Robert Brown (d) James Watson

Sol. (b) The father of genetics is Gregor Mendel. He is known for his groundbreaking work on inheritance patterns in pea plants, where he discovered the fundamental laws of heredity, including the concepts of dominant and recessive traits.

Q.2 Mendel's law of independent assortment holds good for genes situated on the

(a) non-homologous chromosomes (b) homologous chromosomes
(c) extra nuclear genetic element   (d) same chromosomes

Sol. (a) Law of independent assortment states that genes located on non-homologous chromosomes assort independently during meiosis, leading to genetic variation.

Q.3 How many traits were studies in pea plant?

(a) 14 contrasting traits   (b) 7 contrasting traits
(c) 10 traits   (d) 7 traits

Sol. (a) Mendel studied 14 contrasting traits in pea plants, including characteristics like seed shape, color, and plant height.

Q.4 Which of the following represents a pair of contrasting characters?

(a) Alleles   (b) Heterozygous (c) Homozygous (d) Phenotype

Sol. (a) Alleles represent different versions of a gene that can exhibit contrasting characters, such as dominant and recessive traits. For example, an allele for tall (T) and an allele for short (t) represent contrasting characters in plant height.

Q.5 Give the ratio of phenotype in a monohybrid cross.

(a) 1:2:1   (b) 3:1   (c) 1:1:2   (d) 9:3:3:1

Sol. (b) In a monohybrid cross between two heterozygous individuals (Tt × Tt), the phenotypic ratio is typically 3:1.

Q.6 Name the organism which helped in studying sex determining chromosome.

(a) Birds   (b) Grasshopper (c) Humans   (d) Hen

Sol. (b) In grasshoppers, sex is determined by the XX-XY system, where females have two X chromosomes (XX) and males have one X and one Y chromosome (XY).

Q.7 Female heterogamety is shown by

    (a) birds   (b) grasshopper   (c) humans   (d) insects

Sol. (a) Female heterogamety is shown by birds where females produce two different types of sex chromosomes (ZW in birds) and males produce identical sex chromosomes (ZZ in birds).

Q.8 Given the karyotype of klinefelter's syndrome:

    (a) XO, 45   (b) XXX, 47   (c) XXY,47   (d) XYY, 47

Sol. (c) This means that individuals with Klinefelter's syndrome have an extra X chromosome, resulting in a total of 47 chromosomes instead of the typical 46.

Q.9 If a plant heterozygous is self-crossed, the F_2-generation gives dominant, recessive and new variety. It proves the following principle.

    (a) Dominance   (b) Segregation

    (c) Independent assortment   (d) Incomplete dominance

Sol. (d) In incomplete dominance, the heterozygous offspring exhibit an intermediate phenotype, which is different from both the dominant and recessive traits. This creates a new variety or phenotype, showing that neither allele is completely dominant.

☐ Very Short Answer Type

Q.1 State the difference between pleiotropy and polygenic inheritance.

Sol.

Pleiotropy	Polygenic inheritance
When a single gene can exhibit multiple phenotypic expressions it is known as pleiotropy and such a gene is called a pleiotropic gene.	When the traits are controlled by three or more genes they are known as polygenic traits and their inheritance is termed as polygenic inheritance
In most cases it is the effect of a gene on metobolic pathways which contribute towards different phenotypes	It takes into account the influence of environment
For example- Phenylketonuria which occurs in humans.	For example- Human skin colour.

☐ Long Answer Type

Q.1 A. Explain how ABO blood grouping is the example of multiple allelism and co dominance.

   B. Give the karyotype and characteristics of the affected individual with chromosomal disorders.

Sol. A. The ABO blood groups system illustrated multiple allelism because there are three different alleles for the gene controlling blood type. It also demonstrates codominance because the I^A and I^B alleles both express their traits simultaneously when present together.

   B. Chromosomal disorders result from abnormalities in the number or structure of chromosomes. Here's a brief overview of some common chromosomal disorders, including their karyotypes and associated characteristics:

   (i) **Down Syndrome (Trisomy 21)**
   Karyotype: 47,XX,+ 21 (for females) or 47,XY,+ 21 (for males)
   Characteristics
   - Distinctive facial features such as a flat facial profile, slanted eyes, and a small nose.
   - A single transverse palmar crease (simian line).
   - Short stature and a propensity for obesity.
   - Shortened neck, protruding tongue, and hypotonia (decreased muscle tone).
   - Increased risk of congenital heart defects, digestive problems, and early-onset Alzheimer's disease.

   (ii) **Turner Syndrome**
   Karyotype: 45,X (for females, where one X-chromosome is missing or partially missing)
   Characteristics
   - Short stature.
   - Webbed neck and low-set ears.
   - Lack of sexual development and infertility.
   - Heart defects and kidney problems.
   - Normal intelligence, but some individuals may have learning difficulties.

Molecular Basis of Inheritance

CHAPTER 05

Important Points

01 Nucleic acids are long polymers of nucleotides and each nucleotide is composed of three components, *i.e.*

(i) Nitrogenous base (ii) Pentose sugar (iii) Phosphate group

The nitrogen base is further divided into two types.

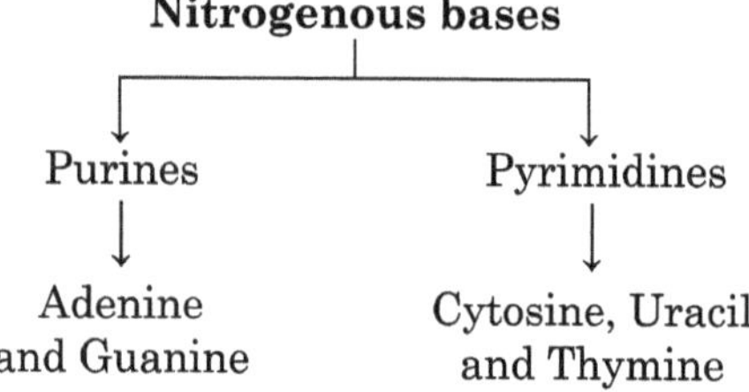

Two types of nucleic acids are found in living organisms, *e.g.*, **Deoxyribonucleic Acid** (DNA) and **Ribonucleic Acid** (RNA) .

02 DNA acts as the genetic material in most of the organisms. It is the information molecule that codes for all the metabolic processes of life.

(i) DNA is a double helix with a sugar-phosphate backbone and nitrogenous bases paired specifically, (adenine with thymine and cytosine with guanine) with the strands oriented in opposite directions.

(ii) DNA is wrapped around histone proteins to form nucleosomes, which then coil into chromatin fibres. These fibres fold into loops and further compact into chromosomes, organising DNA for efficient storage and distribution within the cell nucleus.

(iii) The search for genetic material began with Friedrich Miescher's discovery of DNA in cell nuclei in 1869. Griffith's experiment revealed that a "transforming principle" was transferred between bacteria and resulted in genetic transformation. This was further clarified by Avery, MacLeod, and McCarty in 1944, who identified DNA as the key component responsible for transformation. At last, Hershey and Chase confirmed in 1952 that DNA, not protein, is the genetic material in viruses.

03 **RNA** helps in transfer and expression of information.

It is of three types: *m*RNA, which carries genetic information; *t*RNA, which brings amino acid to the ribosome and *r*RNA, which forms the ribosome and aids in protein synthesis.

It also acts as a genetic material in some viruses. It may also functions as adapter, structural and as a catalytic molecule.

Note Central dogma of molecular biology is the frame work describing the flow of genetic information within a biological system *i.e.*, DNA is replicated, transcribed into *m*RNA, and then translated into proteins.

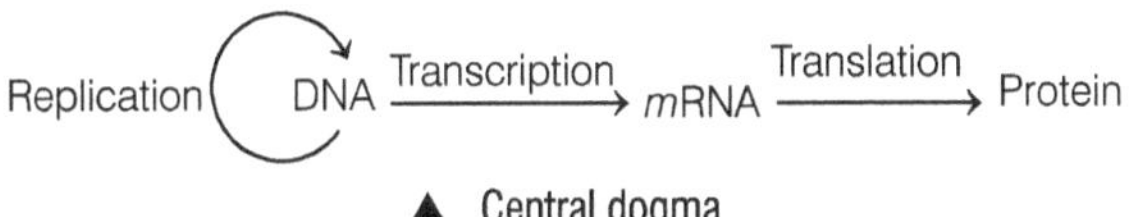

▲ Central dogma

04 **DNA Replication** is the process of copying of DNA to produce two identical molecules. It is semi-conservative in nature, meaning each new DNA molecule contains one original and one newly synthesised strand, as demonstrated by the Meselson-Stahl in 1958. The process of replication is guided by the complementary H-bonding. An enzyme, DNA dependent DNA polymerase uses each DNA strands as template to synthesise new DNA strands. It add nucleotides complementary to the template strand, ensuring accurate DNA replication.

05 **DNA Transcription** is the process where RNA polymerase synthesise a complementary RNA strand from a DNA template.

A segment of DNA that codes for RNA or a polypeptide, can be referred to as a gene.

(i) During **transcription**, a segment of DNA called the transcription unit is used to produce RNA. It includes the promoter, a coding sequence and the terminator.

(ii) In bacteria, the transcribed *m*RNA is functional, hence can directly be translated.

(iii) In eukaryotes, the genes are split. The **coding sequences,** *i.e.* **exons**, are interrupted by **non-coding sequences,** *i.e.* **introns.**

(iv) Introns are removed and exons are spliced back together to produce functional RNA .

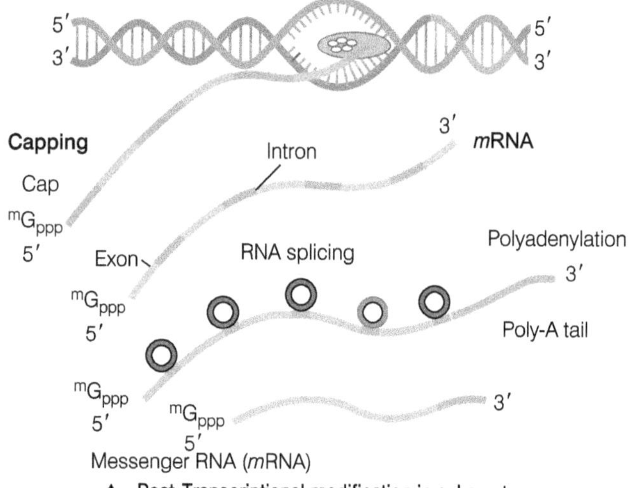

▲ Post-Transcriptional modification in eukaryotes

06 **Genetic Code** is a set of rules that defines how nucleotide sequence in DNA or RNA are translated into amino acid sequences in proteins, with each amino acid specified by a three-nucleotide sequence called a codon.

The genetic code is nearly universal, degenerate unambiguous, non-overlapping and commaless.

07 **Translation** is the process by which ribosomes synthesise proteins by interpreting the *m*RNA sequence and assembling amino acids into a polypeptide chain.

(i) The genetic code is read again on the principle of complementarity by *t*RNA that acts as an adapter molecule. There are specific *t*RNAs for every amino acid.

(ii) The *t*RNA binds to specific amino acid at one end and pairs through H-bonding with codons on *m*RNA via its anticodons. Since, transcription and translation are energetically very expensive processes, these have to be tightly regulated.

08 Regulation of Gene Expression encompasses mechanisms that control transcription, *m*RNA processing and translation to modulate gene activity and protein level. Regulation of transcription is the primary step for the regulation of gene expression. In bacteria, more than one gene are arranged together and regulated in units called **operons.**

Lac **operon** is the prototype operon in bacteria, which codes for genes responsible for the metabolism of lactose. The operon is regulated by the amount of lactose in the medium, where the bacteria are grown.

Therefore, this regulation can also be viewed as regulation of enzyme synthesis by its substrate.

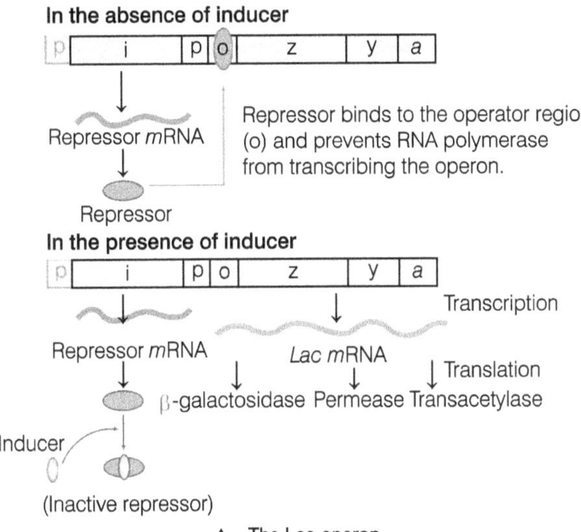

▲ The Lac operon

09 Human Genome Project was a mega project that aimed to sequence every base in human genome, providing a comprehensive reference for genetic research.

10 DNA Fingerprinting is a technique to find out variations in individuals of a population at DNA level. It works on the principle of polymorphism in DNA sequences. It has immense applications in the field of forensic science, genetic biodiversity evolutionary biology as well as in identifying kinship relationship.

Exercises

Question 1 Group the following as nitrogenous bases and nucleosides
Adenine, Cytidine, Thymine, Guanosine, Uracil and Cytosine.

Sol. **Nitrogenous bases** are Adenine, Thymine, Uracil and Cytosine

    Nucleosides are Cytidine and Guanosine.

Question 2 If a double stranded DNA has 20% of cytosine, calculate
the per cent of adenine in the DNA.

Sol. According to chargaff's rule A = T and C = G. Therefore, if C is 20% then G
is also 20%.

Thus,

$$A + T = 100 - (G + C)$$

$$A + T = 100 - 40$$

$$A + T = 60\%$$

Since,   A = T so, both will be 30% each.

Question 3 If the sequence of one strand of DNA is written as follows
5'-ATGCATGCATGCATGCATGCATGCATGC-3'
Write down the sequence of complementary strand in 5' → 3' direction.

Sol. The sequence of complementary strand will be
3'-TACGTACGTACGTACGTACGTACGTACG-5'.

Question 4 If the sequence of the coding strand in a transcription
unit is written as follows

5'-ATGCATGCATGCATGCATGCATGCATGC-3'

Write down the sequence of *m*RNA.

Sol. From the given sequence, the sequence of template strand of DNA can be
reduce as follows:

3'-TACGTACGTACGTACGTACGTACGTACG-5'

Now, RNA strand will be complementary to this template strand, but in
RNA thymine is replace by uracil.

5'-AUGCAUGCAUGCAUGCAUGCAUGCAUGC-3'

Question 5 Which property of DNA double helix led Watson and Crick to hypothesise semi-conservative mode of DNA replication? Explain.

Sol. Watson and Crick hypothesised the semi-conservative mode of DNA replication based on the complementary base pairing and the double-helix structure of DNA, which suggested that each strand of the DNA serves as a template for the synthesis of new complementary strands.

Question 6 Depending upon the chemical nature of the template (DNA or RNA) and the nature of nucleic acids synthesised from it (DNA or RNA), list the types of nucleic acid polymerases.

The various type of nucleic acid polymerases are as follows.

Sol. (i) DNA dependent RNA polymerases for synthesis of RNA from DNA template.

(ii) DNA dependent DNA polymerases for synthesis of DNA from DNA template (Replication).

(iii) RNA dependent DNA polymerase (reverse transcriptase) for synthesis of DNA from RNA template, (Reverse transcription)

Question 7 How did Hershey and Chase differentiate between DNA and protein in their experiment while proving that DNA is the genetic material?

Sol. **Hershey and Chase Experiment**

(i) They grew some bacteriophages on a medium that contained radioactive phosphorus and some in another medium that contained radioactive sulphur.

(ii) Viruses grown in the presence of radioactive phosphorus contained radioactive DNA but not radioactive protein as phosphorus is present only in DNA.

(iii) Viruses grown on radioactive sulphur contained radioactive protein but not radioactive DNA because DNA does not contain sulphur.

(iv) It was found that bacteria infected with bacteriophages containing radioactive DNA were radioactive, indicating that DNA was the material that passed from the virus to the bacteria.

(v) Bacteria that were infected with viruses containing radioactive proteins were not radioactive. This indicates that proteins was not transferred to the bacteria from the viruses.

(vi) This was a clear cut proof that DNA is the genetic material that is passed from virus to bacteria.

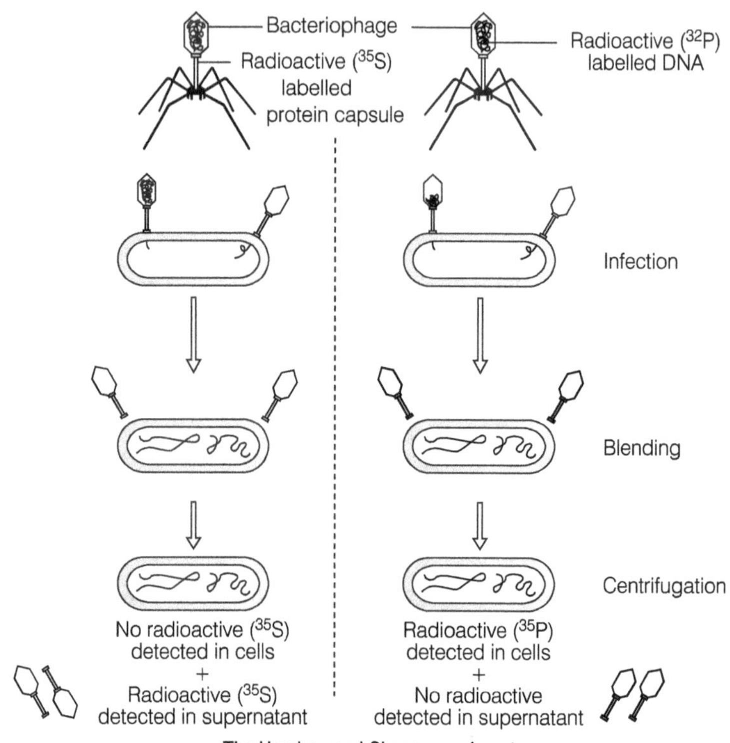

The Hershey and Chase experiment

Question 8 Differentiate between the followings

(a) Repetitive DNA and satellite DNA

(b) *m*RNA and *t*RNA

(c) Template strand and coding strand

Sol. (a) Differences between repetitive DNA and satellite DNA are as follows

S.N.	Repetitive DNA	Satellite DNA
1.	It is the non-coding DNA with multiple copies of identical sequences, which may lie in tandem or interspersed.	It refers to non-coding tandem repeat sequences.
2.	These can be few base pairs to hundreds or thousands of base pairs.	These are generally short sequence repeats (up to 60 base pair long).
3.	During CsCl density gradient analysis, it appears as light bands.	This appears as small dark bands during CsCl density gradient analysis.

(b) Differences between *m*RNA and tRNA are as follows

S.N.	*m*RNA	*t*RNA
1.	It is called messenger RNA and serves as a template for the transcription process.	It is called transfer RNA as it carries amino acids to the site of protein synthesis.
2.	It is single stranded having linear sequence of codons	It has a clover leaf-like structure.
3.	It is synthesised by RNA polymerase II	Synthesised by RNA polymerase III.

(c) Differences between template strand and coding strand are as follows

S.N.	Template Strand	Coding Strand
1.	It has the sequence complementary to the *m*RNA	It has the same sequence as *m*RNA except that thymine in DNA is replaced by uracil in *m*RNA.
2.	It is called anti sense strand.	It is called sense or non-template strand.
3.	It has $3' \rightarrow 5'$ polarity.	It has $5' \rightarrow 3'$ polarity.
4.	It serve as a template for the *m*RNA synthesis during transcription	It serves as a complementary strand of the template strand and does not takes part in transcription.

Question 9 List two essential roles of ribosome during translation.

Sol. The two essential functions of ribosome during translation are as follows:

(i) It serves as platform for protein synthesis by binding *m*RNA in the smaller sub-unit.

(ii) The larger sub-unit has an enzyme peptidyl transferase, which is located on the P-site that facilitates the formation of peptide bonds between amino acids, aiding in the elongation of the polypeptide chain.

Question 10 In the medium, where *E. coli* was growing, lactose was added, which induced the *lac* operon. Then, why does *lac* operon shut down sometime after addition of lactose in the medium?

Sol. The *lac* operon is activated when lactose is added because allolactose, a derivative of lactose, binds to the repressor protein, thus prevents it from binding to the operator region and allowing transcription of the lac genes. Once loctose is used up, allolactose levels drop, the repressor rebinds to the operator, and transcription of the operon is halted.

Question 11 Explain (in one or two lines) the function of the followings

(i) Promoter   (ii) *t*RNA   (iii) Exons

Sol. (i) **Promoter** is an essential component of the transcription unit.

It is located upstream of the coding sequence *i.e.,* adjacent to the 5′ end of the gene. It provides a site for the attachment of transcription factors and RNA polymerase.

(ii) **tRNA** is a small sized RNA molecule that takes part in translation.

It transport specific amino acids to the ribosome during protein synthesis and align them according to the *m*RNA codons, facilitating the assembly of proteins.

(iii) **Exons** are the coding sequences of DNA in eukaryotes that are transcribed into *m*RNA and then translated into proteins.

Question 12 Why is the human genome project called a mega project?

Sol. Human genome project is called a mega project because

(i) it aimed to map and sequence all 3×10^9 base pairs in human genome.

(ii) it involved identifying and analysing over 20,000 human genes.

(iii) it required collaboration among scientists and institutions from many countries.

(iv) it used advanced technology for sequencing and data analysis.

(v) it involves high expenditure of more than 9 billion dollars.

Question 13 What is DNA fingerprinting? Mention its application.

Sol. DNA fingerprinting is the technique used to identify and analyse the variations in various individuals at DNA level. It determines the relationship between two DNA samples by studying the similarity and dissimilarity of VNTRs (Variable number of Tandem Repeats)

DNA fingerprinting has several important applications:

(i) **Forensic science** Identifies individuals in criminal investigations by matching DNA found at crime scenes with suspects.

(ii) **Paternity testing** Establishes biological relationships between parents and children and settles paternity disputes.

(iii) **Genetic research** Helps study genetic variations and hereditary conditions.

(iv) **Missing persons** Assists in identifying missing individuals by comparing their DNA with family members.

Question 14 Briefly describe the following

(a) Transcription   (b) Polymorphism

(c) Translation   (d) Bioinformatics

Sol. (i) **Transcription** is the process by which an RNA molecule is synthesised from a DNA template, where RNA polymerase reads the DNA sequence and produce a complementary RNA strand.

(ii) **Polymorphism** refers to the variation in DNA arising through mutations in both coding and non-coding sequences. Such variations are unique to specific sites of DNA and can occur due to deletion, insertion or substitution of bases. It is the basis for DNA fingerprinting.

(iii) **Translation** is the process of synthesising a polypeptide chain using $mRNA$ as a template, with the help of ribosomal units. The sequence of amino acids is determined by the sequence of triplet codons present on the $mRNA$ transcript.

(iv) **Bioinformatics** is the application of computer science and information technology in the field of biology and medicine. Which deals with handling storing of huge information of genomics as databases, analysing data and creating new knowledge.

DIKSHA APP Questions

☐ Multiple Choice Questions

Q.1 Which one of the following pairs of nitrogenous bases of nucleic acids is wrongly matched with the category mentioned against it?

(a) G, A -- Purines   (b) A, T -- Purines

(c) T, U -- Pyrimidines   (d) U, C -- Pyrimidines

Sol. (b) Adenine is a purine, while thymine is a pyrimidine nitrogen base.

Q.2 Nucleotide arrangement is DNA can be seen by

(a) X-Ray crystallography   (b) electron microscope

(c) ultracentrifuge   (d) light microscope

Sol. (a) X-ray crystallography allows visualization of the 3D arrangement of nucleotides in DNA by analyzing the diffraction pattern of X-rays passed through crystallized DNA.

Q.3 In a DNA percentage of Thymine is 20%. What then will be the percentage of Adenine?

(a) 20%   (b) 40%   (c) 30%   (d) 60%

Sol. (c) According to Chargaff's rule, in DNA, the amount of adenine (A) is always equal to thymine (T). Hence, if thymine is 20%, adenine will also be 20%.

Q.4 In a DNA percentage of Thymine is 20%. What then will be the percentage of Guanine?

(a) 20%   (b) 40%   (c) 30%   (d) 60%

Sol. (c) In DNA, according to Chargaff's rule, the percentage of adenine (A) equals thymine (T), and the percentage of cytosine (C) equals guanine (G). If thymine is 20%, adenine is also 20%. This leaves 60% for guanine and cytosine together. Since they are equal, guanine will be 30%.

Q.5 An octomer of 4 pairs of histones complexed with DNA forms

(a) endosome   (b) nucleosome   (c) mesosome   (d) centromere

Sol. (b) A nucleosome is formed when DNA wraps around an octamer of histone proteins, consisting of two each of histones H2A, H2B, H3, and H4.

Q.6 What are the structures called that given an appearance of "beads on a string" in the chromosomes when viewed under an electron microscope?

(a) Genes   (b) Nucleotides   (c) Nucleosomes (d) Base pairs

Sol. (c) Under an electron microscope, nucleosomes appear as "beads on a string." These beads are DNA wrapped around histone protein octamers, linked by linker DNA.

Q.7 Semi conservative replication of DNA was first demostrated in

(a) *Escherichia coli*   (b) *Streptococcus pneumoniae*
(c) *Salmonella typhimurium*   (d) *Drosophila melanogaster*

Sol. (a) The semi-conservative replication of DNA was first demonstrated by Meselson and Stahl in E. coli using isotopes of nitrogen.

Q.8 *E. coli* fully labelled with ^{15}N is allowed to grow in ^{14}N medium. The Two strands of DNA molecule of the first generation bacteria have

(a) different density and do not resemble parent DNA
(b) different density, but resemble parent DNA
(c) same density and resemble parent DNA
(d) same density out do not resemble parent DNA

Sol. (a) First generation DNA has one strand with 15N (parental) and one strand with 14N (newly synthesized). This hybrid DNA has a density intermediate between 15N and 14N DNA, and it does not match the density of the original parent DNA.

Q.9 Taylor conducted experiments to prove semi-conservative mode of DNA replication on

(a) *Vinca rosea*   (b) *Vicia faba*
(c) *Drosophila melanogaster*   (d) *E.coli*

Sol. (b) Taylor used root tips of *Vicia faba* (broad bean) to demonstrate the semi-conservative replication of DNA.

Q.10 During transcription, the DNA site at which RNA polymerase binds is called

(a) promoter   (b) regulator   (c) receptor   (d) enhancer

Sol. (a) The promoter is the DNA sequence where RNA polymerase binds to initiate transcription.

Q.11 Which one of the following is not a part of a transcription unit in DNA?

(a) Inducer   (b) Terminator   (c) Promoter   (d) Structural gene

Sol. (a) An inducer is a molecule that regulates gene expression by activating transcription, but it is not a part of the transcription unit.

Q.12 If one strand of DNA has the nitrogenous base sequence as ATCTG, what would be the complementary RNA strand sequence?

(a) TTAGU   (b) UAGAC   (c) AACTG   (d) ATCGU

Sol. (b) In RNA, adenine (A) pairs with uracil (U) instead of thymine (T), and cytosine (C) pairs with guanine (G). Therefore, the RNA sequence will be UAGAC.

Q.13 DNA-dependent RNA polymerase catalyses transcription from one strand of DNA, which is called

(a) template strand (b) coding strand (c) alpha strand (d) anti strand

Sol. (a) DNA-dependent RNA polymerase catalyzes transcription using the template strand of DNA to synthesize a complementary RNA strand.

Q.14 DNA elements which can switch their positions are called

(a) cistrons   (b) transposons   (c) exons   (d) introns

Sol. (b) Transposons, also known as "jumping genes," are DNA elements that can move or switch positions within the genome.

Q.15 In eukaryotic cell transcription, RNA splicing and RNA capping take place inside the

(a) ribosomes   (b) nucleus   (c) dictysomes   (d) ER

Sol. (b) Both RNA splicing and RNA capping occur in the nucleus before the RNA is transported to the cytoplasm for translation.

Q.16 Removal of introns and joining of exons in a defined order during transcription is called

(a) looping   (b) inducing   (c) slicing   (d) splicing

Sol. (d) Splicing is the process by which non-coding regions are removed and coding regions are joined together in *m*RNA.

Q.17 Which of the following reunites the exon segments after RNA splicing?

(a) RNA polymerase   (b) RNA primase

(c) RNA ligase   (d) RNA proteoses

Sol. (c) RNA ligase joins the exons together after the introns have been removed during RNA splicing, forming the mature mRNA.

Q.18 In the genetic code dictionary, how many codons are used to code for all the 20 essential amino acids?

(a) 20   (b) 64   (c) 61   (d) 60

Sol. (b) The genetic code uses 64 codons (combinations of three nucleotides) to code for all 20 amino acids.

Q.19 In the genetic dictionary, there are 64 codons as

(a) 64 amino acids are to be coded

(b) 64 types of tRNA are present

(c) There are 44 nonsense codons and 20 sense codons

(d) Genetic code is triplet

Sol. (d) The 64 codons in the genetic code arise from the triplet nature of the code, where each codon consists of three nucleotides, resulting in 64 possible combinations (43).

Q.20 Which one of the following is a start codon?

(a) UAA   (b) UAG   (c) AUG   (d) UGA

Sol. (c) AUG codes for the amino acid methionine and signals the beginning of translation in protein synthesis.

Q.21 Which one of the following serves as a terminal codon?

(a) UAG   (b) AGA   (c) AUG   (d) GCG

Sol. (a) UAG is one of the three stop codons in the genetic code, signaling the end of protein synthesis.

Q.22 What would happen if in a gene encoding a polypeptide of 50 amino acids, 25th codon (UAU) is mutated to UAA?

(a) A polypeptide of 24 amino acids will be formed.

(b) Two polypeptides of 24 and 25 amino acids will be formed.

(c) A polypeptide of 49 amino acids will be formed

(d) A polypeptide of 25 amino acids will be formed.

Sol. (a) UAA is a stop codon, which signals the termination of translation, causing the polypeptide to end prematurely.

Q.23 In a mutational event, when adenine is replaced by guanine, it is a case of

(a) frame shift mutation   (b) transcription
(c) transition   (d) transversion

Sol. (c) A transition is a type of mutation where a purine is replaced by another purine (adenine to guanine) or a pyrimidine is replaced by another pyrimidine (cytosine to thymine).

Q.24 If the DNA codons are ATG ATG ATG and a cytosine base in inserted at the beginning, then which of the following will result?

(a) CAT GAT GAT G   (b) A nonsense mutation
(c) C ATG ATG ATG   (d) CA TGA TGA TG

Sol. (a) Insertion of a cytosine at the beginning shifts the reading frame, causing a frameshift mutation.

Q.25 In three dimensional view a molecule of *t*RNA is

(a) L − shaped   (b) S − shaped   (c) Y − shaped   (d) E − shaped

Sol. (a) In a three-dimensional view, a *t*RNA molecule adopts an L-shape due to its structure, where one end holds the amino acid and the other binds to the *m*RNA during translation.

Q.26 Ribosomal RNA is actively synthesised in

(a) lysosomes   (b) nucleolus   (c) nucleoplasm   (d) ribosomes

Sol. (b) Ribosomal RNA is synthesized in the nucleolus, where it combines with proteins to form ribosomal subunits.

Q.27 A complex of ribosomes attached to a single of RNA is called

(a) polypeptide (b) okazaki fragment (c) polysome   (d) polymer

Sol. (c) A polysome is a complex of multiple ribosomes attached to a single *m*RNA molecule, synthesising proteins simultaneously.

Q.28 The process of translation is

(a) Ribosome synthesis   (b) Protein synthesis
(c) DNA synthesis   (d) RNA synthesis

Sol. (b) Transcription is a biological process that converts messenger RNA into proteins in a cells cytoplasm.

Q.29 In protein synthesis, the polymerisation of amino acids involves 3 steps. Which one of the following is not involved in polymerisation of protein?

(a) Termination   (b) Initiation
(c) Elongation   (d) Transcription

Sol. (d) Transcription is the process of RNA synthesis, not involved in the polymerisation of proteins, which occurs during translation.

Q.30 The equivalent of a structural gene is

(a) muton   (b) cistron   (c) operon   (d) recon

Sol. (b) A cistron is the functional unit of a gene that codes for a specific polypeptide, making it equivalent to a structural gene.

Q.31 In operon concept, regulator gene functions as

(a) Inhibitor   (b) Repressor   (c) Regulator   (d) All of these

Sol. (b) The regulator gene produces a repressor protein that can bind to the operator, inhibiting transcription of the structural genes.

Q.32 Out of the following, which non human model's genome has been sequenced?

(a) *Ascaris lumbricoides*   (b) *Caenorhabditis elegans*
(c) *Rosa indica*   (d) *Corvus splendens*

Sol. (b) The genome of *Caenorhabditis elegans*, a nematode, has been sequenced and is widely used as a model organism in genetic research.

Q.33 The method of DNA sequencing was developed by

(a) Frederick Sanger   (b) Hershey & Chase
(c) Watson & Crick   (d) Erwin Chargaff

Sol. (a) Frederick Sanger developed the method of DNA sequencing, known as the Sanger method, which was instrumental in decoding DNA sequences.

Q.34 One of the most frequently used techniques in DNA fingerprinting is

(a) VNTR   (b) SSCP   (c) SCAR   (d) AFLP

Sol. (a) Variable Number Tandem Repeats (VNTR) is one of the most frequently used techniques in DNA fingerprinting, as it involves analysing the variations in the number of tandem repeats in specific regions of DNA.

Q.35 The technique of DNA fingerprinting involves

(a) Northern Blotting   (b) Southern Blotting
(c) Eastern Blotting   (d) Western Blotting

Sol. (b) Southern blotting is a technique used in DNA fingerprinting to detect specific DNA sequences by transferring DNA fragments onto a membrane and hybridizing them with labeled probes.

☐ Short Answer Type

Q.1 State the role of enzyme helicase and ligase in the process of replication.

Sol. The enzyme, helicase is responsible for breaking the hydrogen bonds that hold DNA strands together. As a result, it facilities the formation of a replication fork whereas DNA ligase helps in joining of the DNA strands (okazaki fragments) during replication by catalysing the formation of a phosphodiester bond between the two nucleotides.

Q.2 Packaging of eukaryotic DNA is a complex process. Comment.

Sol. In eukaryotes, the packaging of DNA is a complex process as the positively charged, basic proteins called histones, are organised to form a unit of eight molecules called the histone octamer on which the negatively charged DNA is wrapped around to form a structure called nucleosome. These nucleosomes are packed into thread like structures called chromatin fibres, which condense to form chromosomes during mitosis.

☐ Long Answer type

Q.1 (a) AUG is a dual function codon. Justify
(b) Explain the process of translation.

Sol. (a) AUG is a dual function codon i.e. it codes for methionine and it also acts as initiation codon.

(b) Translation is the process by which a cell converts genetic information from *m*RNA into a corresponding amino acid sequence to build proteins. The process of translation is completed in the following steps

  (i) **Initiation**
- During this process activations of amino acid takes place followed by charging of *t*RNA in which amino acid binds to the *t*RNA.
- *m*RNA binds to a ribosome.
- The start codon AUG present on *m*RNA is recognised only by the charged *t*RNA

  (ii) **Elongation**
- During the process of elongation the ribosome moves one codon to another along with *m*RNA.
- *t*RNA molecule with complementary anticodons bring amino acids to the ribosome.
- Amino acids are linked together by peptide bonds to form a polypeptide chain.

  (iii) **Termination**
- In this process ribosome reaches a stop codon on the *m*RNA
- The polypeptide chain is released and the ribosomal subunits and *m*RNA disassemble.

Evolution

Important Points

01 **Evolutionary Biology** is the study of history of life forms on earth.

02 **Origin of Life** refers to the process by which life began on earth. The main theories proposed to explain the origin of life encompass :

  (i) Theory of abiogenesis proposes that life arose spontaneously from non-living matter through natural processes.

  (ii) Theory of biogenesis states that living organisms originate only from pre-existing living organisms.

  (iii) Theory of chemical evolution suggests that life originated from simple chemical compounds through a series of complex reactions, leading to the formation of organic molecules and eventually living organisms.

The theory of chemical evolution is supported by findings such as the Miller Urey experiment, which illustrate that organic molecule can emerge from simple inorganic compounds under prebiotic conditions.

03 **Evidence of Evolution** reveals how living organisms have transformed and adapted over time. These are as follows.

  (i) **Palaeontology** Study of fossils (remains of hard parts of life forms found in rocks).

    Rocks of different ages contain fossils of different life forms (that probably died during the formation of the particular sediment).

(ii) **Comparative anatomy and morphology** Comparison of internal structures and external features shows similarities and differences among the organisms of today and those of earlier times.

    (a) **Homologous organs** These organs have same structures, but different function in various organisms.

        Homology indicates common ancestry and is based on **divergent evolution,** which represents the evolutionary pattern in which species sharing common ancestry become more distant due to differential selection pressure.

        Example

        Whales, bats, cheetah and humans (all mammals) share similarities in the pattern of bones of forelimbs but these forelimbs perform different functions in different animals.

        In plants also, the thorn and tendrils of *Bougainvillea* and *Cucurbita* represent homology.

    (b) **Analogous organs** These organs perform similar function, but have different internal (anatomical) structure.

        They are a result of **convergent evolution**, which means different structures evolving for the same function and hence having similarity.

        Example

        Eye of the *Octopus* and mammals, Flippers of penguins and dolphins as well as sweet potato (root modification) and potato (stem modification).

(iii) **Embryological evidence** Ernst Haeckel proposed that the similarity in embryonic development among vertebrates, such as the presence of gill slits, provide evidence for evolution. However, karl Ernst von Baer refuted this by arguing that embryos do not pass through adult stages of other species.

(iv) **Evolution by natural selection** shows how species adapt to environmental changes. Some examples are as follows

    • In England, factory pollution darkened tree bark, making light coloured moths more visible to predators. Dark-coloured moths, being better camouflaged, have higher survival rate and reproduce more successfull, increasing their number in polluted area.

- Similarly, excess use of herbicides, pesticides, etc., has resulted in selection of resistant varieties in a much lesser time scale.
- This is also true for the microbes against, which antibiotics or drugs are used.
- These are examples of evolution by anthropogenic action. This also tells us that the evolution is chance events in nature and chance mutation in the organisms.

04 Adaptive Radiation This is process of evolution of different species in a given geographical area starting from a point and literally radiating to other areas of geography (habitats).

(i) Small black birds, later called Darwin's finches, are perfect example of adaptive radiation. From the original seed-eating features, later many other forms with altered beaks arose, enabling them to become insectivorous and vegetarian finches.

(ii) Another example is Australian marsupials. A number of marsupials, each different from the other evolved from an ancestral stock, but all within the Australian island continent.

(iii) When more than one adaptive radiations appeared to have occurred in an isolated geographical area (representing different habitats), one can call this **convergent evolution**.

(iv) Placental mammals in Australia also exhibit adaptive radiation in evolving into forms 'similar' marsupial (*e.g.*, placental wolf and Tasmanian wolf marsupial).

05 Biological Evolution Evolution by Natural Selection, probably started when cellular forms of life with minor differences in metabolic capability originated on the earth.

(i) Darwin's theory of evolution emphasizes natural selection.

(ii) Nature selects the fittest, which refers to the individuals that are better adapted to survive in an otherwise hostile environment.

(iii) Adaptive ability is inherited. It has a genetic basis. Fitness is the end result of the ability to adapt and get selected by nature.

(iv) Those favoured by nature survive and reproduce, passing this traits to the next generation, resulting in gradual evolution of species.

(v) Species with shorter life cycles, like microbes, can evolve rapidly. In contrast, organisms with longer life sporesachet take millions of years for similar evolutionary changes.

(vi) Even before Darwin, Lamarck proposed that evolution occured through the use and disuse of organs, using giraffes' neck elongation as an example. However, this idea is no longer accepted by scientists today.

(vii) **Hugo de Vries** based on his work on evening primrose brought forth the idea of mutation- large differences arising suddenly in population.

(viii) Evolution for Darwin was gradual, while de Vries believed mutation caused speciation.

06 Hardy-Weinberg Principle It states that allele and genotype frequencies in a population remain constant from generation to generation in the absence of evolutionary forces, such as mutation, migration, genetic drift, and natural selection.

The Hardy-Weinberg principle is expressed by the following formula

- Genotype frequencies $p^2 + 2pq + q^2 = 1$
- Allele frequencies $p + q = 1$

Here, p is the frequency of the dominant allele, q is the frequency of the recessive allele, p^2 represents the frequency of the homozygous dominant genotype, $2pq$ represents the frequency of the heterozygous genotype, and q^2 represents the frequency of the homozygous recessive genotype.

07 A Brief Account of Evolution Life on earth began with simple cells around 2000 million years ago slowly, single celled organisms evolve into multi-cellular forms. By 500 million years ago, (mya) invertebrates appeared and jawless fish evolved about 350 mya. Plants were the first to colonise land, followed by amphibians, which evolved into reptiles.

Dinosaurs dominated for about 200 million years before their sudden disappearance 65 million years ago. Mammals, evolving from small shrew-like creatures, eventually replaced reptiles and diversified into various forms, including aquatic species.

08 **Origin and Evolution of Man** Human evolution began with primitive ancestors and progressed to modern humans with advanced abilities and culture. The different stages of human evolution are as follows:

(i) *Dryopithecus* **and** *Ramapithecus* **(15 mya)** Early primates, *Dryopithecus* was more ape-like, while *Ramapithecus* had more human-like features.

(ii) *Australopithecus* **(2 mya)** Used stone tools, mainly ate fruit.

(iii) *Homo habilis* First human-like species, brain size 650-800 cc, did not eat meat.

(iv) *Homo erectus* (1.5 mya) Larger brain (900 cc), likely ate meat, fossils found in Java.

(v) *Neanderthals* **(100,000-40,000 years ago)** Large brain (1400 cc), used hides for protection and buried their dead.

(vi) *Homo sapiens* Emerged in Africa, spread globally, developed art and agriculture about 10,000 years ago, marking the start of settled civilisations.

Exercises

Question 1 Explain antibiotic resistance observed in bacteria in light of Darwinian selection theory.

Sol. Darwinian selection theory states that individuals with favourable variations are better adapted than individuals with less favourable variation. It means that nature selects the individuals with useful variation as these individuals are better evolved to survive in the existing environment. A classic example of this process is antibiotic resistance in bacteria. When bacterial population was grown on an agar plate containing antibiotic penicillin, the colonies that were sensitive to penicillin died, whereas one or few bacterial colonies that were resistant to penicillin survived.

This is because these bacteria had undergone chance mutation, which resulted in the evolution of a gene that made them resistant to penicillin drug. Hence, the resistant bacteria multiplied quickly as compared to non-resistant (sensitive) bacteria, thereby increasing their number.

Question 2 Find out from newspapers and popular science articles any new fossil discoveries or controversies about evolution.

Sol. New fossils discoveries are as follows

New Discoveries in Dinosaur Fossils

- **Fossilised soft tissues** Scientists have continued to make exciting discoveries of fossilised soft tissues in dinosaur remains. For example, in 2021, researchers found that some dinosaur fossils preserved traces of blood vessels and proteins, providing new insights into the physiology and appearance of these ancient creatures.
- **Feathered dinosaurs** Ongoing discoveries in China, particularly in the Liaoning Province, have provided new evidence of feathered dinosaurs. These findings help clarify the evolution of feathers and their role in dinosaurian thermoregulation and eventually in the evolution of flight.

Controversies in Evolutionary Theory

- **Human evolution and interbreeding** The study of ancient DNA has shown that early humans interbred with neanderthals and denisovans. Recent research suggests that these interbreeding events had significant effects on the immune system and other traits in modern humans, fueling debates about the extent and impact of these interactions.
- **The role of epigenetics** There's ongoing debate about the role of epigenetics in evolution. Some scientists argue that epigenetic changes (modifications that affect gene expression without altering the DNA sequence) might play a role in evolutionary processes, challenging traditional Darwinian views that emphasise genetic mutations.

Question 3 Attempt giving a clear definition of the term species.

Sol. A species is one or more populations of individuals that can interbreed under natural conditions and produce fertile offsprings.

Question 4 Try to trace the various components of human evolution (Hint : Brain size and function, skeletal structure, dietary preference, etc.).

Sol.   **A. Brain size** It increased gradually along with evolution. The brain capacity of *Australopithecus* −500 cc, *Homo habilis* −700 cc, *Homo erectus* −800 – 1300 cc, *Homo sapiens sapiens* −1450 cc.

    B. Skeletal structure

      (i) *Dryopithecus* was ape-like, without brow ridges, had semierect posture, and prognathous face (having a projecting jaw) ,

      (i) *Ramapithecus* had jaws and teeth like humans (small canines and large molars), prognathous face and walked on legs.

      (ii) *Australopithecus* had erect posture, human like teeth, was without chin, with brow ridges, and had prognathous face.

      (iv) *Homo habilis* walked nearly erect, had human like teeth, with brow ridges, face was slightly prognathous.

      (v) *Homo erectus* had erect posture, prognathous face, with projecting brow ridges, small canines and large molar teeth and had small chin.

      (vi) *Homo sapiens* had four curves in the vertebral column, orthognathous face (without projecting jaw), forehead broad, chin well developed, walked on sole.

    C. Dietary preference *Dryopithecus* and *Ramapithecus* were herbivores, *Australopithecus* and *Homo habilis* were carnivores, *Homo erectus* and *Homo sapiens sapiens* were omnivores.

Question 5 Find out through internet and popular science articles whether animals other than man has self-consciousness.

Sol.   Chimpanzees are animals other than humans who have self-conciousness.

Question 6 List 10 modern day animals and using the internet resources link it to a corresponding ancient fossil. Name both.

Sol.

Modern Day Animal	Ancient Fossil
Dog	*Leptocyon*
Birds	*Archaeopteryx*
Camel	*Procamelus*
Elephant	*Moeritherium*
Reptiles	*Seymouria*
Vertebrates	*Ostracoderms*
Frogs, toads and salamander	*Labyrinthodontia*
Horse	*Pilohippus*
Octopus	*Belemnite*
Man	*Ramapithecus*

Question 7 Practise drawing various animals and plants.

Sol. Student do it yourself.

Question 8 Describe one example of adaptive radiation.

Sol. The process of evolution of different species in a geographical area starting from a point and literally radiating to other areas of geography (habitats) is called adaptive radiation. Darwin's finches represent one of the best examples of this phenomenon. Darwin observed that in Galapagos island many varieties of finches evolved on the island itself.

They once had a common ancestor but with evolution they modified into different types according to their food habits. From the original seed-eating features, many other forms with altered beaks arose, enabling them to become insectivorous and vegetarian finches.

Question 9 Can we call human evolution as adaptive radiation?

Sol. Adaptive radiation is a phenomenon in which different species in a geographical area starting from a point are evolved and they all literally spread out to other habitats. Human evolution is not the case of adaptive radiation. Human evolution is a gradual and step by step process, which took place slowly in time.

Question 10 Using various resources such as your school Library or the internet and discussions with your teacher, trace the evolutionary stages of any one animal, say horse.

Sol. Early Ancestors
- **Eohippus (Hyracotherium)**
  Features Eohippus were small, dog-sized with multiple toes, browsing herbivore.
- **Mesohippus (Evolved from Eohippus)**
  Features Mesohippus were slightly larger, with three toes on the front feet and longer legs. adapted to more open environments.
- **Merychippus (Evolved from Mesohippus)**
  Features Merychippus were large size, more developed hoof, adaptation to grazing on grasses.
- **Pliohippus (Evolved from Merrychippus)**
  Features Pliohippus were more similar to modern horses, with a single dominant toe, early form of the modem hoof.
- **Genus Equus (Evolved from Pliohippus)**
  Features Equus are modern horses with single, fully developed hoof, large size, and adaptation to a grazing diet.

DIKSHA APP Questions

☐ Multiple Choice Questions

Q.1 Earth was supposed to be formed

    (a) 4.5 billion years ago   (b) 2 billion years ago

    (c) 5.4 billion years ago   (d) 8.6 billion years ago

Sol. (a) Earth is believed to have formed approximately 4.5 billion years ago.

Q.2 Early thinkers thought that units of life called spores were transferred to different plants including earth. This theory of evolution is known as

    (a) Spontaneous generation   (b) Panspermia

    (c) Chemical evolution   (d) Natural

Sol. (b) Panspermia is the theory according to which life or its building blocks were transported to Earth from outer space, possibly via spores or meteorites.

Q.3 The experiment that simulated conditions thought to be present on the early earth

    (a) Hershey-Chase experiment   (b) Geiger-Marsden experiment

    (c) Miller-Urey experiment   (d) Schiehallion experiment

Sol. (c) It demonstrated that amino acids, the building blocks of life, could be synthesised from simple gases (like methane, ammonia, hydrogen, and water) when exposed to electric sparks, simulating lightning in Earth's early atmosphere.

Q.4 Organic compounds first evolved on Earth required for origin of life were

    (a) proteins and Amino acids   (b) proteins and Nucleic acids

    (c) urea and Amino acids   (d) urea and Nucleic acids

Sol. (b) Proteins are essential for catalysing biochemical reactions and building cellular structures, while nucleic acids store and transmit genetic information necessary for life.

Q.5 The force that initiates evolution is ………

    (a) variation   (b) mutation   (c) extinction

    (d) adaptation

Sol. (a) The force that initiates evolution is variation.

Q.6 Which one of the following experiments suggests that simplest living organisms could not have originated spontaneously from non-living matter?

(a) Microbes did not appear in stored meat
(b) Meat was not spoiled, when heated and kept sealed in a vessel
(c) Larva could appear in decaying organic matter
(d) Microbes appeared form unsterilised organic matter

Sol. (b) Microbes were killed by heating the meat and the sealed vessel formed a closed system wherein the new microbes could not come in contact with the nutrient medium and hence no spoilage of meat.

Q.7 On the Origin of Species was written by ………. .

(a) Alfred Wallace
(b) Ludmila Kuprianova
(c) Mikhail A.Fedonkin
(d) Charles Darwin

Sol. (d) "On the Origin of Species" was written by Charles Darwin. It was published in 1859 and introduced the theory of evolution by natural selection, revolutionizing the understanding of biology and the origin of species.

Q.8 Select the correct statement from the following:

(a) Fitness is the end result of the ability to adapt and gets selected by nature
(b) Darwinian variations are small and directionless
(c) Mutations are random and directional
(d) All mammals except whales and camels have seven cervical vertebrae

Sol. (a) This aligns with Darwin's theory of natural selection, where fitness refers to an organism's ability to survive and reproduce in its environment, with advantageous traits being passed on to the next generation.

Q.9 According to Oparin, which of the following was not present in early earth?

(a) Methane   (b) Hydrogen
(c) Water vapour   (d) Oxygen

Sol. (d) Oparin proposed that early Earth had a reducing atmosphere composed of gases like methane, hydrogen, and water vapor, but lacked free oxygen.

Q.10 The idea of Natural selection as the fundamental process of evolutionary changes was reached

(a) independently by Charles Darwin and Alfred Russel Wallace
(b) by Charles Darwin
(c) by Alfred Russel Wallace
(d) by Lamarck

Sol. (a) The idea of natural selection as fundamental process of evolutionary changes was reached independently by Darwin and Russel in 1859.

Q.11 When did the dinosaurs die off?

(a) 105 million years ago
(b) 65 million years ago
(c) 75.5 million years ago
(d) 1 million years ago

Sol. (b) Dinosaurs went extinct around 65 million years ago at the end of the Cretaceous period, due to a mass extinction event likely caused by a combination of factors, including an asteroid impact and volcanic activity.

Q.12 A study of fossils in different sedimentary layers indicates the .... period in which they existed.

(a) geographical
(b) geological
(c) mythological
(d) historical

Sol. (b) A study of fossils in different sedimentary layers indicates the geological period in which they existed. The study showed that life forms varied over time and certain life forms are restricted to certain geological time spans.

Q.13 The eyes of *Octopus* and eye of a cat show similar function, but show different patterns of structure. This is an example of

(a) homologous organ evolved due to convergent evolution
(b) homologous organ evolved due to divergent evolution
(c) analogous organ evolved due to convergent evolution
(d) analogous organ evolved due to divergent evolution

Sol. (c) Analogous structures are a result of convergent evolution i.e. different structures evolving for the same function and hence having similarity.

Q.14 Examples of a homologous organ

(a) the arm of a human, wing of a bird
(b) wing of an insect, wing of a bird
(c) leg of a dog, leg of a spider
(d) sweet potato, potato

Sol. (a) The arm of a human and wing of a bird is an example of homologous organs. When the organs resemble each other by structure, but functions differ from each other, then the organs are referred to as Homologous organs.

Q.15 When two species of same genealogy take up different function as a result of adaptation, the phenomenon is termed
(a) microevolution
(b) divergent evolution
(c) convergent evolution
(d) co-evolution

Sol. (b) Divergent evolution occurs when two species of a common ancestry develop different traits or functions due to adapting to different environments or ecological niches.

Q.16 Which type of selection is industrial melanism observed in moth?
(a) stabilising
(b) directional
(c) disruptive
(d) artificial

Sol. (b) Industrial melanism in moths is an example of directional selection, where darker moths became more prevalent due to better camouflage in polluted environments.

Q.17 Appearance of antibiotic-resistant bacteria is an example of
(a) adaptive radiation
(b) transduction
(c) pre-existing variation in the population
(d) divergent evolution

Sol. (c) The appearance of antibiotic-resistant bacteria is an example of pre-existing variation where mutations confer resistance, and over time, these genes spread, making the entire population resistant.

Q.18 Evolution of different species in a given area starting from a point and spreading to other geographical areas is known as
(a) Migration
(b) Divergent evolution
(c) Adaptive radiation
(d) Natural selection

Sol. (c) Adaptive radiation is when a species spreads to new areas and changes to form new species.

Q.19 After 1920, the dark-winged moth population increased in England. This is an example of

(a) convergent evolution   (b) anthropogenic action
(c) adaptive radiation   (d) saltation

Sol. (b) The increase in the dark-winged moth population in England after 1920 is an example of industrial melanism, an anthropogenic action caused by industrial pollution, which favored darker moths due to their better camouflage.

Q.20 Which condition can be explained by Lamarckism?

(a) Giraffes got their long neck   (b) Humans lost their tall
(c) Humans became bipedal   (d) Extinction of Dinosaurs

Sol. (a) According to Lamarck's theory, giraffes developed long necks because their ancestors stretched their necks to reach higher food, and this acquired trait was passed on to future generations.

Q.21 Evolution according to de Vries is due to single step large mutation. The theory is known as ………. .

(a) genetic drift   (b) natural selection
(c) adaptive radiation   (d) saltation

Sol. (d) Saltation is the theory that evolution occurs through large, sudden mutations rather than gradual changes.

Q.22 Sometimes due to change in allele frequency in a new population, a different species is formed. The original drifted population is called ………. .

(a) founder   (b) marsupials
(c) synapsids   (d) tracheophyte

Sol. (a) The original drifted population is called a founder population. This occurs when a small group of individuals from the original population establishes a new population, and over time, genetic drift leads to the formation of a different species.

Q.23 Due to continental drift, pouched mammals of Australia survived because of

(a) competition with other existing species
(b) chance mutation
(c) lack of competition
(d) genetic recombination

Sol. (c) Due to continental drift, Pouched mammals (marsupials) from Australia survived due to lack of competition from any other mammals, as they were geographically isolated.

Q.24 In Hardy-Weinberg equation, the frequency of heterozygous individual is represented by

(a) p^2 (b) $2pq$

(c) q^2 (d) pq

Sol. (b) In the Hardy-Weinberg equation, the frequency of heterozygous individuals is represented by $2pq$, where p is the frequency of the dominant allele and q is the frequency of the recessive allele.

Q.25 In a population of 1000 individuals, 360 belongs to genotype AA, 480 at Aa and the remaining 160 to aa. Based on this data the frequency of allele A in the population is

(a) 0.4   (b) 0.5

(c) 0.6   (d) 0.7

Sol. (c) The frequency of allele A is calculated as 0.6 using the formula $p = (2AA + Aa) / (2N)$, where AA = 360, Aa = 480, and N = 1000.

The frequency of allele A is calculated as $p = (2 \times 360 + 480) / (2 \times 1000)$

$$= 0.6$$

Q.26 Change of frequency of alleles in a population results in evolution. This statement is proposed in

(a) Darwin's theory   (b) Hardy-Weinberg principle

(c) Lamarck's theory   (d) de Vries theory

Sol. (b) In Hardy-Weinberg equilibrium, allele frequencies in a population are stable and constant from generation to generation that causes changes in allele population resulting in evolution.

Q.27 Tendency of a population to remain in genetic equilibrium may be disturbed by

(a) random mating   (b) lack of mutation

(c) lack of migration   (d) lack of random mating

Sol. (d) The tendency of a population to remain in genetic equilibrium can be disturbed by factors such as lack of random mating, mutation, migration, genetic drift, and natural selection.

Q.28 The earliest geological time period among the following is … .

(a) triassic   (b) permian

(c) jurassic   (d) quaternary

Sol. (b) The earliest geological time period among the following is Permian.

Q.29 Some of the land reptiles went back to water to evolve into fish like reptiles like .... probably 200 million years ago.

(a) Ichtyosaurs   (b) Therapsids

(c) Shrews   (d) Sea cows

Sol. (a) Land reptiles that went back into the water and evolved into fish-like reptiles probably around 200 million years ago are known as marine reptiles, such as ichthyosaurs. These reptiles adapted to an aquatic lifestyle while retaining their reptilian characteristics.

Q.30 The cranial capacity of Java man was about

(a) 560 cc   (b) 1000 cc

(c) 1300 cc   (d) 900 cc

Sol. (d) The cranial capacity of Java Man (*Homo erectus*) is approximately 900 to 1,100 cubic centimeters.

Q.31 The animals called .... evolved into amphibians

(a) lobefins   (b) salamander

(c) synapsids   (d) *Ramapithecus*

Sol. (a) The animals that evolved into amphibians are lobe-finned fish. These fish adapted to life on land, leading to the evolution of early amphibians around 370 million years ago.

Q.32 Nutritionally Australopithecines were

(a) omnivorous   (b) carnivorous

(c) herbivorous   (d) frugivorous

Sol. (d) Australopithecus were likely frugivores, primarily eating fruits, along with some other plant-based foods.

Q.33 Common ancestor of Apes and man is

(a) Sauropsids   (b) *Homo habilis*

(c) *Dryopithecus*   (d) *Australopithecines*

Sol. (c) *Dryopithecus* is considered as the common ancestor of the great apes and man. These are believed to have lived during Miocene(about 16 million years ago).

Q.34 Evolution of man is believed to have taken place in

(a) Central America   (b) Australia

(c) Asia   (d) Africa

Sol. (d) The evolution of humans is believed to have taken place in Africa, with early hominins, such as *Australopithecus*, evolving around 4 to 6 million years ago. The most widely accepted theory is that modern humans, *Homo sapiens*, evolved in Africa and later migrated to other parts of the world.

Q.35 Jurassic period of the Mesozoic era characterised by

(a) dinosaurs become extinct and angiosperms appear

(b) radiation of reptiles and origin of mammal like reptiles

(c) gymnosperms are dominant plants and first birds appear

(d) flowering plants and first dinosaurs appear

Sol. (c) During the Jurassic period of the Mesozoic era, dinosaurs dominated, toothed birds like *Archaeopteryx* appeared, marsupials evolved from prototheria, and gymnosperms thrived.

Q.36 Which one of the following is closest relative of man?

(a) Chimpanzee (b) Orangutan

(c) Gorilla (d) Gibbon

Sol. (a) Chimpanzees are the closest relatives of humans, supported by immunological evidence, DNA-DNA hybridization, DNA sequencing, chromosomal analysis, and protein sequences.

Q.37 The extinct human who lived 1,00,000 to 40,000 years ago, in Europe, Asia and parts of Africa, with short stature, heavy eye brows, retreating fore heads, large jaws with heavy teeth, stocky bodies, a lumbering gait and stooped posture was

(a) Cro-Magnon humans (b) *Ramapithecus*

(c) *Homo habilis* (d) Neanderthal man

Sol. (d) The Neanderthal human, extinct between 100,000 to 40,000 years ago, had a stocky body, heavy eyebrows, large jaws, and a stooped posture, and lived in Europe, Asia, and parts of Africa.

Q.38 The most accepted line of descent in human evolution is

(a) *Australopithecus* → *Ramapithecus* → *Homo sapiens* → *Homo habilis*

(b) *Homo erectus* → *Homo habilis* → *Homo sapiens*

(c) *Ramapithecus* → *Homo habilis* → *Homo erectus* → *Homo sapiens*

(d) *Australopithecus* → *Ramapithecus* → *Homo erectus* → *Homo habilis* → *Homo sapiens*

Sol. (c) The most accepted line of descent in human evolution is *Ramapithecus* → *Homo habilis* → *Homo erectus* → *Homo sapiens*.

Q.39 Neanderthal man differs from modern man in

    (a) receding jaws   (b) protruding Jaws

    (c) could make good tools   (d) could make cave art

Sol. (b) Neanderthal man differs from modern humans in features like a stocky build, heavy brow ridges, protruding jaws, as well as a smaller brain size and different limb proportions.

☐ Very Short Answer Type

Q.1 Define convergent evolution. Give any two examples with reference to animals.

Sol. Convergent evolution is the process in which organisms that are not closely related independently evolve similar features. Examples for convergent evolution are as follows-

Example 1 Wings of butterfly and of birds looks like analogous structures as they are anatomically different but they perform similar functions.

The eyes of a octopus and mammals are considered analogous structures, they perform similar function (vision) but have evolved independently from different ancestor.

Q.2 A. Explain industrial melanism as the example of natural selection.

    B. Give any two factors that affect the Hardy-Weinberg principle.

Sol. A. Industrial melanism is an example of natural selection, a fundamental mechanism of evolution. Before industrialisation, it was observed that there were more white-winged moths on trees than dark-winged or melanised moths. In 1920, there were more dark-winged moths in the same area, i.e., the proportion was reversed. The explanation put forth for this observation was that 'predators will spot a moth against a contrasting background'. During post industrialisation period, the tree trunks became dark due to industrial smoke and soots. Under this condition the white-winged moth did not survive due to predators, while dark-winged or melanised moth survived.

    B. There are various factors that are known to affect Hardy-Weinberg equilibrium. These are gene migration or gene flow, genetic drift, mutation, genetic recombination and natural selection.

Human Health and Disease

CHAPTER 07

Important Points

01 Health could be defined as a state of complete physical, mental and social well-being.

02 Health is affected by

(i) **Genetic disorders** deficiencies with which a child is born and deficiencies/defects which the child inherits from parents from birth.

(ii) Infections.

(iii) Life style including eating and drinking habits, rest and exercise we give to our bodies, habits that we have or do not have, etc.

03 Balanced diet, personal hygiene, regular exercise and good thinking are very important to achieve good physical and mental health.

04 Drug and alcohol abuse affect our health adversely.

05 Disease refers to a state of the body when functioning of one or more organs or systems of the body is adversely affected. It is characterised by various signs and symptoms. Disease causes suffering, pain and both physical and mental debilitation.

06 Diseases can be

(i) **Infectious** that can be transmitted from one person to another and therefore are very common.

Example Cold, flu, AIDS, etc.

(ii) **Non-infectious** that can not be transmitted.

Example Arthritis, diabetes, cancer, etc.

   (iii) **Congenital** Which are present in the human being since birth and occurs due to mutation and chromosomal aberration of colour blindness, Down's syndrome, etc.

   (iv) Acquired are diseases develop after birth of influenza, hepatitis.

07 Disease causing **agents** like bacteria, viruses, fungi, protozoans, helminths, etc. are called **pathogens**.

08 Most parasites are therefore pathogens as they cause harm to the host by living in or on them.

09 Pathogens enter the body by various routes and multiply in the host body.

10 Pathogens adapt to life within the environment of the host. For example, the pathogens that infect gastrointestinal system are adapted to survive in the stomach at low pH and resist the action of various digestive enzymes.

11 Common Human Diseases

   (i) **Typhoid** fever caused by a pathogenic bacterium *Salmonella typhi*. It enters the small intestine through contaminated food and water and migrates to other organs through blood. Common **symptoms** of typhoid include high fever (39°-40°C) weakness, stomach pain, constipation,headache and loss of appetite.

   (ii) **Pneumonia** is caused by bacteria like *Streptococcus pneumoniae* and *Haemophilus influenza*.

They infect the alveoli (air filled sacs) of the lungs, that get filled with fluid leading to severe problems in respiration. **Pneumonia symptoms** include fever, chills, cough, headache and in severe cases, gray or bluish lips and fingernails.

Infection spreads Bacterial infections like dysentery, plague or diphtheria spread *via* infected droplets or shared utensils.

   (iii) **Common cold** is caused by rhino viruses.

They infect the nose and respiratory passage, but not the lungs. **Symptoms** of common cold causes nasal congestion sore throat, cough headache and tiredness.

Infection spreads through exposure to droplets or contact with contaminated objects like cups, books or keyboards.

(iv) **Malaria** is caused by a protozoan *Plasmodium (P. vivax, P. malariea* and *P. falciparum).*

Of these, malignant malaria caused by *Plasmodium falciparum* is the most serious one and can be fatal. **Malaria symptoms** include fever, chills, sweating, headache and muscle pain.

Infection spreads through female *Anopheles* mosquito that acts as the vector (transmitting agent) as well as serves as a host for its development up to a stage. The malarial parasite requires two hosts-human and mosquitoes, to complete its life cycle, as shown in the diagram below.

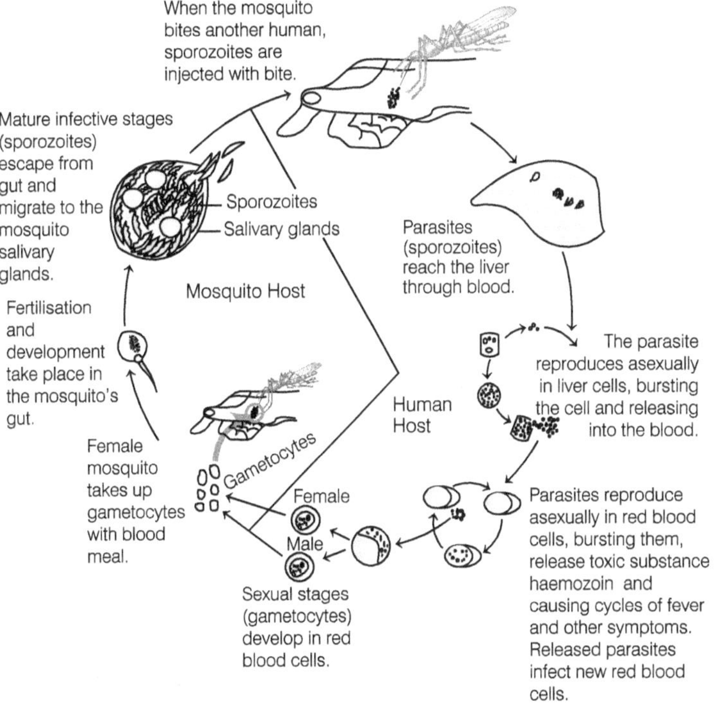

▲ Stages in the life cycle of *Plasmodium*

(v) **Amoebiasis** (amoebic dysentery) is caused by *Entamoeba histolytica,* a protozoan parasite in the large intestine of human.

Symptoms include constipation, abdominal pain, cramps and bloody mucus in stools. Houseflies transmit parasites from faeces to food, contaminating water and food as the main source of infection.

(vi) **Ascariasis** is caused by *Ascaris lumbricoides* (round worm) an intestinal parasite.

    Symptoms include internal bleeding, muscle pain, fever, anaemia and intestinal blockage.

    Infection spreads parasite eggs in faces contaminate water, food and soil, infecting healthy individuals.

(vii) **Elephantiasis** or **Filariasis** *Wuchereria* (*W. bancrofti* and *W. malayi*), the filarial worms. Elephantiasis symptoms include chronic inflammation and deformities in the limbs and genital organs.

(viii) **Ringworms** infections are caused by fungi belonging to the genera *Microsporum, Trichophyton* and *Epidermophyton*. These fungi thrive in skin folds because of warmth and moisture.

    Symptoms include dry, scaly lesions on the skin, nails and scalp.

Infection spreads from soil or from contaminated towels, clothes or even the comb of infected individuals.

12 Maintaining personal and public hygiene are crucial for preventing disease, including cleanliness, safe food, water and proper waste disposal.

13 **Immunity** It is the ability of an organism conferred by the immune system to resist and fight diseases. Imminunity is of two types.

(i) **Innate immunity** is a non- specific defence present at birth, providing barriers to prevent foreign agents from entering the body. It consist of four types of barriers. The four barriers include physical barriers (skin), physiological barrier (stomach acid), cellular barrier (white blood cells) and cytokine barriers (Interferon from, virus infected cells).

(ii) **Acquired immunity** is pathogen-specific and based on memory. The first encounter of pathogen triggers a weak **primary response,** while later encounters with the same pathogen cause a stronger **secondary response.** Primary and secondary immune responses are carried out by B-lymphocytes and T-lymphocytes in the blood. B-lymphocytes produce antibodies to fight pathogens, while T-lymphocytes help B-cells to make them.

14 **Antibodies** have four peptide chains, two light and two heavy chains (H_2L_2). IgA, IgM, IgE, and IgG are the various types of antibodies. The antibody-mediated response, found in the blood, is called **humoral immunity.** The second type is **cell-mediated immunity** (CMI).

15 **Active and Passive immunity** Active immunity occurs when the body produces its own antibodies after exposure to antigens, either through vaccination or natural infection, and takes time to develop. Passive immunity is when ready-made antibodies are given directly to the body for immediate protection.

16 Vaccination and Immunisation

Vaccination	Immunisation
The process involves using vaccines to trigger an immune response to protect against infections/ diseases	The process of making one resistant to an infectious disease usually through vaccination
It is usually injected or administered orally	It is not administered in any way. The body develops resistence from vaccines

17 Allergies
(i) The exaggerated response of the immune system to certain antigens in the environment (pollen, dust mites, molds, cloth fibers, animal hair, etc.) is called allergy.

(ii) The substances to which such an immune response is produced are called **allergens**.

18 **Autoimmune Disease** Memory based immunity allows the body to distinguish between foreign organisms and its own cells. In autoimmunity, the immune system attacks the body's own cells, causing diseases like rheumatoid arthritis.

19 **Immune System in the Body**
The human immune system consists of lymphoid organs and lymphatic tissues.

Lymphoid organs are where lymphocytes originate, mature, and proliferate. Primary organs like bone marrow and thymus produce and mature lymphocytes, while secondary organs like the spleen, lymph nodes, and tonsils allow lymphocytes to interact with antigens and become active. The **bone marrow** produces all blood cells, including lymphocytes, while the **thymus** helps mature T-lymphocytes. The **spleen** filters blood, trapping microorganisms and storing red blood cells. **Lymph nodes** trap antigens in lymph, activating lymphocytes for-immune response. Mucosa-associated **lymphoid tissue** (MALT) is found in the linings of major tracts (respiratory,digestive, and urogenital) and makes up about 50% of lymphoid tissue in the body.

20 **AIDS or Acquired Immuno Deficiency Syndrome** means deficiency of immune system, acquired during the lifetime of an individual, indicating that it is not a congenital disease. Syndrome means a group of symptoms.

It is caused by the Human Immuno Deficiency Virus (HIV), a retrovirus, which has an envelope enclosing the RNA genome.

(i) HIV is transmitted through sexual contact, contaminated blood transfusion, shared needles and from mother to child *via* the placenta.

(ii) **HIV/AIDS** spreads only through body fluids.

There is always a time-lag between the infection and appearance of AIDS symptoms. This period may vary from a few months to many years (usually 5-10 years).

Many people remain asymptomatic for long time and can infect other people through sexual contact.

(iii) **Life cycle of HIV virus** The life cycle of the HIV virus is shown in the diagram below.

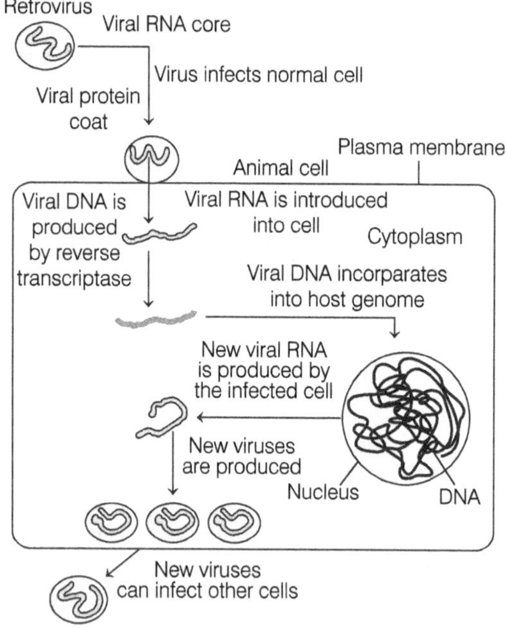

▲ Infected cell can survive, while viruses are being replicated and released. Replication of retrovirus.

(iv) **The Enzyme-Linked ImmunoSorbent Assay** (ELISA) is a common diagnostic test for AIDS. Anti- retroviral drugs can prolong life but cannot prevent death.

(v) **Prevention of AIDS** As AIDS has no cure, prevention is the best option.

HIV often spreads through conscious behaviours, through it can also be transmitted *via* blood transfusions or from mother to newborn due to poor monitoring

21 Cancer is a major cause of death all over the globe. It is caused by the breakdown of normal regulatory mechanisms of cell growth.

(i) Normal cells show a property called **contact inhibition** (they stop growing on coming in contact with other cells).

(ii) Cancer cells, however, lose this property and continue to divide giving rise to masses of cells called **tumours**.

(iii) Tumours are of two types–**benign** and **malignant**.

A **benign tumor** is non- cancerous, grown slowly and doesn't spread to other parts of the body.

A malignant tumor is cancerous, grows rapidly, invades surrounding tissues and can spread to other parts of the body through metastasis.

22 Causes of Cancer Cancer is caused by the transformation of normal cells into carcinogens (Cancerous cell) due to physical, chemical or biological agents. Carcinogens include ionising radiation (like x-rays γ-rays) UV radiation, chemical carcinogens in tobacco smoke. Some genes called oncogenes when activated can also lead to cancer.

23 Cancer Detection and Diagnosis Early cancer detection through biopsy, histopathology, blood tests and imaging techniques like x-rays, CT and MRI is crucial for successful treatment.

24 Treatment of Cancer Cancer treatment involves surgery radiation (target tumors), chemotherapy (drugs to bill cancer) and immutherapy(α- interferon) boosts the immune system to destroy tumors.

25 **Drugs and Alcohol Abuse**
  (i) **Opioids,** like heroin (diacetylmorphine), derived from the poppy plant, *Papaver somniferum,* bind to opioid receptors in the central nervous system and gastrointestinal tract. Heroin, a white, odorless, bitter crystalline compound, is usually snorted or injected. As a depressant, it slows down body functions.
  (ii) **Cannabinoids,** derived from *Cannabis sativa,* interact with brain receptors. The plant's flower tops, leaves, and resin are used to make marijuana, hashish, charas, and ganja, which affect the cardiovascular system and are typically inhaled or ingested. Some athletes also abuse cannabinoids.
  (iii) **Cocaine,** derived from the *Erythroxylum coca* plant, stimulates the central nervous system, causing euphoria and increased energy, but excessive use can lead to hallucinations. It is usually snorted. Other hallucinogenic plants include Atropa *belladonna* and *Datura.*

26 **Tobacco,** used for over 400 years, contains nicotine, which raises blood pressure and heart rate. Smoking is linked to lung, bladder, and throat cancers, bronchitis, heart disease, and gastric ulcers, while chewing tobacco increases the risk of oral cancer. Smoking also raises carbon monoxide levels, reducing oxygen in the body.

27 Adolescence (12-18 years) is a time of growth, where curiosity, stress, and peer pressure often lead to drug and alcohol experimentation. Media influence and unstable family environments further contribute to substance abuse. Initially driven by curiosity, later use is often to escape problems.

Prevention and Control
  (i) Avoid peer pressure
  (ii) Education and counselling
  (iii) Seek help from parents, teachers or professionals.

Exercises

Question 1 What are the various public health measures, which you would suggest as safeguard against infectious diseases?

Sol. Public health measures to safe guard against various diseases are

(i) Creating awareness in people through proper education. People should know about health, its importance and how it can be achieved through personal cleanliness and hygiene and various preventive measures.

(ii) Vaccination/Immunisation is a preventive measure that can help

(a) eradicate infections.

(b) lower the severity of infections.

(c) Decrease the chronic effects of infection.

(iii) Sanitation and proper disposal of waste.

(iv) Eradication of various vectors like flies, mosquitoes, mice, lice, etc.

(v) Provision of clean drinking water.

Question 2 In which way has the study of biology helped us to control infectious diseases?

Sol. Study of biology has helped us to control infectious diseases in following ways.

(i) discover the causative agents and vectors.

(ii) understand the course of infections and diseases.

(iii) understand the signs and symptoms.

(iv) develop specific diagnostic tests.

(v) develop the preventive (vaccinations) and curative (antibiotics) measures.

(vi) The life cycle of the pathogen is studied.

(vii) Alternate and reservoir hosts are known.

Question 3 How does the transmission of each of the following diseases take place?

(a) Amoebiasis (b) Malaria

(c) Ascariasis (d) Pneumonia

Sol. (a) **Amoebiasis** Through contaminated food and water.

(b) **Malaria** Through the bite of female *Anopheles* mosquito.

(c) **Ascariasis** Through taking contaminated food and water.

(d) **Pneumonia** Droplets from the sputum of the patient.

Question 4 What measure would you take to prevent water-borne diseases?

Sol. To prevent water borne diseases, following measures are required

    (i) Drinking water should be clean, free from contamination. This could be achieved by filtration, boiling or sedimentation and chemical treatment of water.

    (ii) Water resources/reservoirs should be periodically de-contaminated/disinfected.

    (iii) Water should not be allowed to stand for long to become breeding pools for insect vectors.

    (iv) Prevention of passage of garbage and sewage into the water bodies.

    (v) Standards practices of hygiene should be strictly maintained in public catering.

Question 5. Discuss with your teacher what does 'a suitable gene' means, in the context of DNA vaccines.

Sol. Suitable gene would mean 'specific gene' (which is a segment of DNA) that can be modified and put into the host so that it produces specific protective proteins (antibodies) to fight against infection or disease causing agent.

Question 6 Name the primary and secondary lymphoid organs.

Sol.   (i) Primary lymphoid organs are bone marrow and thymus.

    (ii) Secondary lymphoid organs are

        (a) spleen   (b) lymph nodes   (c) tonsils

        (d) Peyer's patches of small intestine   (e) appendix

Question 7 The following are some well known abbreviations, which have been used in this chapter. Expand each one to its full form.

    (a) MALT   (b) CMI   (c) AIDS

    (d) NACO   (e) HIV

Sol.   (a) MALT—Mucosa Associated Lymphoid Tissue

    (b) CMI—Cell Mediated Immunity

    (c) AIDS—Acquired Immuno Deficiency Syndrome

    (d) NACO—National AIDS Control Organisation

    (e) HIV—Human Immunodeficiency Virus.

Question 8 Differentiate the following and give examples of each

(a) Innate and acquired immunity

(b) Active and passive immunity

Sol. (a) Innate and Acquired Immunity

Innate Immunity	Acquired Immunity
1. It is a non-specific type of defence	1. It is pathogen-specific
2. It is present at the time of birth	2. It develops during one's lifetime
3. It does not have a memory	3. It is characterised by memory
4. It works by providing various types of barriers	4. It works by producing primary and secondary responses, which are carried out by the help of B- lymphocytes and T-lymphocytes
5. Examples- Interferons protect non-infected cells from further viral infection and mucus coating of epithelium living that traps microbes entering the body.	5. Example- Development of natural immunity in a person recently recovered from a disease and the resistance induced by vaccination

(b) Active and Passive Immunity

Active Immunity	Passive Immunity
1. It refers to the response in which antibodies are produced in the host body on actual exposure to living or dead antigens.	1. It refers to the introduction of ready made antibodies directly into the host body to protect against foreign agents.
2. Actual infection or vaccination induce active immunity.	2. The foetus receives some antibodies from its mother, through the placenta during pregnancy and the infant receives them from the yellowish fluid called colostrum secreted by mother during the initial days of lactation.

Question 9 Draw a well-labelled diagram of an antibody molecule.

Sol.

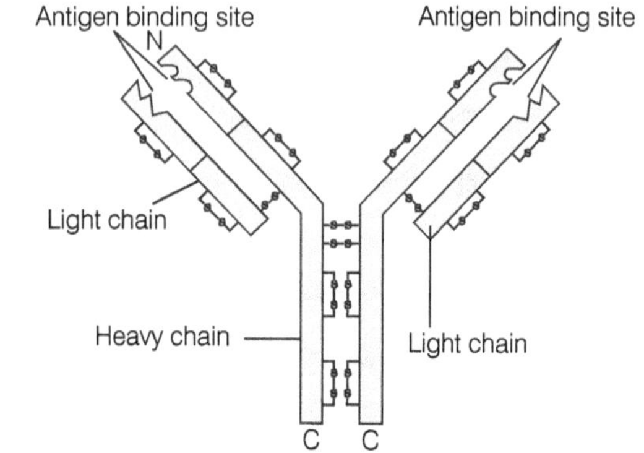

Structure of an antibody molecule

Question 10 What are the various routes by which transmission of human immunodeficiency virus takes place?

Sol.   Various routes for entry of HIV virus are
  (i) sexual contact with the infected person.
  (ii) through placenta (from infected mother to foetus).
  (iii) transfusion of infected blood or blood products.
  (iv) sharing infected needles and syringes to inject drugs.

Question 11 What is the mechanism by which the AIDS virus causes deficiency of immune system of the infected person?

Sol.   (i) When the HIV virus enters the human body, it attacks the macrophages. Here, the RNA genome of the virus replicates with the help of enzyme reverse transcriptase and forms viral DNA.
  (ii) This viral DNA gets incorporated into host cell's DNA.
  (iii) It directs the infected cells to produce virus particles.
  (iv) The macrophages continue to produce virus acting like an HIV factory. HIV enters into helper T-lymphocytes.
  (v) It replicates and produces progeny viruses.
  (vi) The progeny viruses released in the blood.
  (vii) They attack other helper T-lymphocytes.
  (viii) This is repeated leading to a progressive decrease in the number of helper T-lymphocytes in the body of the infected person.

  During this period, the person suffers from bouts of fever, diarrhoea and weight loss. The patient becomes so immuno-deficient and is completely unable to protect themselves from infections.

Question 12 How is a cancerous cell different from a normal cell?

Sol. Cancer cell is different from normal cells in the sense that it
   (i) loses the property of contact inhibition.
   (ii) continues to grow and divide in unregulated and uncontrolled manner
   (iii) produces masses of cells called tumours.
   (iv) show metastasis.

Question 13 Explain what is meant by metastasis?

Sol. Metastasis means dissemination (spread) of cancerous cells from original site to other body sites through blood or other tissue fluids. This property is exhibited by malignant tumours which divide uncontrollably, resulting in the formation of a mass of cells called tumour. Some cells from the tumour enter the blood and reach to different parts of the body to form new tumours.

Question 14 List the harmful effects caused by alcohol/drug abuse.

Sol. The adverse effects of drugs and alcohol abuse are
   (i) low to moderate doses can cause reckless behaviour, vandalism and violence, depression, fatigue, weight fluctuations, etc.
   (ii) excessive doses of drugs may lead to coma and death due to respiratory failure, heart failure or cerebral haemorrhage.
   (iii) a combination of different drugs or alcohol mixed with drugs results in overdosing and even death.

Question 15 Do you think that friends can influence one to take alcohol/drugs? If yes, how may one protect himself/herself from such an influence?

Sol. Yes, sometimes peer group can put you on the wrong track and can cause wrong influence. But one can always protect himself/herself by
   (i) reminding oneself of the disastrous effects of alcohol or drugs.
   (ii) realising that one time try can lead to more often intake.
   (iii) resisting temptation or pressure by strong will.
   (iv) changing the company of a peer group that consume drugs.
   (v) seeking help from parents/counselors.
   (vi) seeking medical and professional intervention.

Question 16 Why is that once a person starts taking alcohol or drugs, it is difficult to get rid of this habit? Discuss it with your teacher.

Sol. It is difficult to get rid of this habit, because these substances are addictive and once one starts having unpleasant feelings or withdrawal symptoms like nausea, etc. The mind loses control and all one can think of is taking the addictive substance. Repeated intake increases the tolerance level of the receptors in the body, resulting in more consumption.

Question 17 In your view what motivates youngsters to take to alcohol or drugs and how can this be avoided?

Sol. Probably the 'motivation' to take alcohol or drugs comes from

(i) curiosity to experience the effect.

(ii) foolishness to try to prove oneself in front of the peers.

(iii) wrongly taking it as an excuse to escape from reality.

(iv) wrong thinking that one time 'try' is not going to do any harm.

(v) to overcome stress, tepression, frustration, etc. Measures/ways to avoid alcohol or drugs are avoiding undue perpressure, educating and awareness about its ill effects. Seeking medical and professional help if required.

DIKSHA APP Questions

☐ Multiple Choice Questions

Q.1 Typhoid disease is caused by

(a) *Plasmodium*   (b) *Salmonella*

(c) *Wuchereria*   (d) *Entamoeba histolytica*

Sol. (b) Typhoid disease is caused by the bacterium *Salmonella typhi*.

Q.2 The rupture of RBCs is associated with release of toxic substance Hemozoin causes chill fever in

(a) pneumonia   (b) malaria   (c) filariasis   (d) ascariasis

Sol. (b) The rupture of red blood cells (RBCs) and the release of the toxic substance hemozoin causes chills and fever in malaria, which is caused by the *Plasmodium* parasite.

Q.3 Acid in stomach and saliva in mouth

(a) physical immunity barrier   (b) cellular immunity barrier
(c) physiological immunity barrier (d) cytokine immunity barrier

Sol. (c) The acid in the stomach and saliva in the mouth act as physiological barriers in the immune system, helping to prevent the entry of pathogens.

Q.4 Primary lymphoid organ is

(a) spleen   (b) tonsils

(c) bone marrow   (d) lymph node

Sol. (c) Among spleen, lymph nodes, bone marrow, and tonsils, the primary lymphoid organs are bone marrow and thymus (though the thymus was not listed). These are where lymphocytes are produced and mature.

Q.5 HIV enters into which type of cells to produce progeny virus

(a) B- lymphocytes (b) T- lymphocytes

(c) RBC (d) Platelets

Sol. (b) HIV enters T-lymphocytes (a type of white blood cell) and uses these cells to produce more viruses, weakening the immune system over time.

Q.6 Time lag between the infection & appearance of AIDS symptoms

(a) 5-10 months   (b) 6-11 months   (c) 5-20 years   (d) 5-10 years

Sol. (b) The time lag between HIV infection and the appearance of AIDS symptoms can range from 5 to 10 years, although it varies depending on factors like treatment and individual health.

Q.7 Orcogenic viruses have genes called

(a) proto oncogene (b) viral oncogene

(c) cellular oncogene (d) non-cellular oncogene

Sol. (b) Oncogenic viruses have genes known as viral oncogenes, which can promote the development of cancer by altering the normal growth of cells.

Q.8 Computed tomography uses X-rays to generate

(a) uni-dimensional image of internals of an object

(b) two-dimensional image of internals of an object

(c) three-dimensional image of internals of an object

(d) normal image of internals of an object

Sol. (c) Computed tomography (CT) uses X-rays to generate three-dimensional images of the body's internal structures.

Q.9 Chronic use of drugs and alcohol specially causes

(a) cirrhosis (b) cardiac muscles damage

(c) pulmonary system damage (d) gametogenesis

Sol. (a) Chronic use of drugs and alcohol can lead to cirrhosis, a condition characterised by scarring of the liver, which can eventually cause liver failure.

Q.10 Nowadays which is being usually abused by some sportspersons

(a) opioids (b) cannabinoids (c) cocaine (d) Smack

Sol. (b) Cannabinoids are usually abused by sports persons for their relaxing effects or pain management, despite impairing

☐ Short Answer Type

Q.1 What do you understand by the "memory" of the immune system? Write the name of that principle which is based on this property?

Sol. Memory of the immune system refers to the ability of the immune system to respond more rapidly and effectively to pathogens that have been encountered previously. Subsequent encounter with the same pathogen elicits a highly intensified response. Acquired immunity is characterised by memory. Principle of immunisation or vaccination is based on this property of the immune system.

Q.2 What happens when HIV virus enters into T lymphocytes of a person?

Sol. After HIV enters into helper T-Iymphocytes (T_H),the RNA genome of the virus replicates to form viral DNA with the help of the enzyme reverse transcriptase and replicates to produce progeny viruses. The progeny viruses are released in the blood and attack other helper T-Iymphocytes. This is repeated leading to a progressive decrease in the number of helper T-Iymphocytes in the body of the infected person. During this period, the person suffers from bouts of fever, diarrhoea and weight loss.

☐ Long Answer Type

Q.1 What certain sportspersons do to enhance their performance? Write four side effects of the use of anabolic steroid on both male and female. (Sportspersons) .

Sol. Sportspersons take steroid to enhance their performance.

Side Effects of Anabolic Steroid Use

In Males:

1. **Hormonal Imbalance** Reduced sperm production, leading to infertility and decreased libido.
2. **Gynecomastia** Development of breast tissue.
3. **Aggression** Increased likelihood of aggressive behavior and mood swings.
4. **Cardiovascular Issues** Increased risk of heart disease, high blood pressure, and cholesterol imbalance.

In Females:

1. **Virilisation** Development of male characteristics such as deepened voice, facial hair, and enlarged clitoris.
2. **Menstrual Irregularities** Disruption of the menstrual cycle and potential infertility.
3. **Skin Issues** Acne and oily skin.
4. **Hair Loss** Increased risk of thinning hair and male-pattern baldness.

Microbes in Human Welfare

CHAPTER 08

Important Points

01 Microbes are present everywhere, *i.e.*, in soil, water, air, inside plants and animal bodies including humans.

02 Microbes thrive in extreme environments like deep inside the geysers, deep soil, thick snow layers and highly acidic conditions.

03 Microbes are diverse and can be found in nature in various forms, such as, Protozoa, Bacteria, Fungi, Animal and plants viruses, Viroids, Prions (proteinacious infectious agents).

04 Bacteria and fungi form visible colonies on nutrient media. Such cultures are useful in studies on microorganisms.

05 Some microbes cause infections and diseases in human beings, animals and plants. But most of the microbes are useful in many ways.

06 **Microbes in Household Products** We use microbes or their products daily. Some common examples are as follows.

    (i) Lactic Acid Bacteria (LAB) turn milk into curd, enhancing its vitamin B_{12} content and aiding digestion by preventing harmful microbes.

    (ii) Bacteria ferment dosa and idli dough, producing CO_2 to make it puffed up. Yeast (*Saccharomyces cerevisiae*) ferments bread dough. Microbes also make 'toddy' from palm sap and ferment foods like fish, soybeans and bamboo shoots.

(iii) **Cheese,** is also made by using microbes. Different varieties of cheese have their characteristic texture, flavour and taste, coming from the microbes used. *e.g., Propionibacterium sharmanii* creates the hole in swiss cheese.

The **'Roquefort cheese'** are ripened by growing a specific fungi *Penicillium roqueforti* on them, which gives them a particular flavour.

07 Microbes in Industrial Products Microbes are used in industries to produce valuable products like beverages and antibiotics, typically grown in large vessels called fermentors.

08 Fermented Beverages Yeast (*Saccharomyces cerevisiae*), used in bread-making, ferments malted cereals and fruit juices to produce ethanol, which is the basis for beverages like wine, beer, whisky, brandy, and rum. Wine and beer are made without distillation, while whisky, brandy, and rum are produced by distillation of the fermented broth.

09 Antibiotics is a greek word which translates to 'against life'.

Alexander Fleming discovered **penicillin** from *Penicillium notatum* mould, which inhibited bacterial growth. Its full potential was realised by **Ernest Chain** and **Howard Florey**, and it was widely used in World War II. They won the Nobel Prize in 1945 for the discovery.

After penicillin, other antibiotics were purified from microbes. They have been crucial in treating deadly diseases like plague, whooping cough, diphtheria, and leprosy, saving millions of lives. Today, antibiotics are essential in modern medicine.

10 Chemicals, Enzymes and other Bioactive Molecules Microbes are also used for commercial and industrial production of

(i) Organic acids   (ii) Bioactive molecules (iii) Enzymes

S.N.	Microbe	Product
1.	*Aspergillus niger* (a fungus)	Citric acid
2.	*Acetobacter aceti* (a bacterium)	Acetic acid
3.	*Clostridium butylicum* (a bacterium)	Butyric acid
4.	*Lactobacillus* (a bacterium)	Lactic acid
5.	(Yeast) *Saccharomyces cerevisiae*	Ethanol

Microbes are also used for production of enzymes and some bioactive molecules

S.N.	Mirobial product	Use
1.	Lipases	In detergent formulations and to remove oily stains from laundry
2.	Pectinases and Proteases	To clarify commercial juices
3.	Streptokinase produced by bacterium streptococces	As a 'clot buster' for removing blood clots from blood vessels of patients
4.	Cyclosporin a Produced by fungus *trichoderma polystporum.*	As an immunosuppressive agent in organ transplant patients
5.	Statins produced by yeast *Monascus purpureus.*	As blood-cholesterol lowering agents

11 Microbes in Sewage Treatment Sewage, primarily made up of human excreta, contains organic matter and harmful microbes. It cannot be directly released into water bodies and must be treated in Sewage Treatment Plants (STPs)using natural heterotrophic microbes. The treatment occurs in two stages to reduce pollution.

(i) **Primary treatment** It involves physical removal of large and small particles, from the sewage through filtration and sedimentation.

All solids that settle down, form the **primary sludge** and the supernatant forms the effluent.

The effluent from the primary settling tank is taken for secondary treatment.

(ii) In secondary (biological) treatment, primary effluent is aerated in large tanks to promote the growth of aerobic microbes, which consume organic matter and reduce the Biochemical Oxygen Demand (BOD). BOD measures the oxygen consumed by microbes in water, indicating the level of organic pollution. The treatment continues until the BOD is significantly reduced.

After reducing the BOD, the effluent is passed into a settling tank where bacterial flocs form **activated sludge.** Some sludge is recycled to the aeration tank, while the rest is sent to anaerobic digesters, where bacteria produce **biogas** (methane, hydrogen sulphide, and carbon dioxide) used as energy. The treated effluent is then released into natural water bodies.

12 The **Ministry of Environment and Forests** launched the **Ganga** and **Yamuna Action Plans** to reduce pollution in these rivers by building sewage treatment plants for discharging only treated sewage.

13 **Biogas,** mainly composed of methane, is produced by microbes, particularly methanogens like *Methanobacterium,* which thrive in anaerobic environments. These bacteria, found in sewage sludge and the rumen of cattle, break down cellulose, aiding cattle nutrition. Cattle dung, rich in methanogens, is used to generate biogas, also known as **gobar gas.**

14 **Microbes as Biocontrol Agents** Biocontrol uses biological methods to manage plant diseases and pests, offering an alternative to chemical insecticides and pesticides, which are toxic and pollute the environment, soil, water, and crops.

Biological control manages pests "through natural predation rather than chemicals. Organic farmers use a balanced ecosystem to keep pests manageable. For example, ladybirds control aphids, dragonflies target mosquitoes, and *Bacillus thuringiensis* controls butterfly caterpillars on crops. The fungus *Trichoderma* is used to treat plant diseases, while baculoviruses, particularly from the *Nucleopolyhedrovirus* genus, target specific insect pests without harming other organisms.

15 **Microbes as Biofertilisers** Biofertilisers are organisms that enhance soil nutrients, including bacteria, 'fungi, and cyanobacteria.

Rhizobium bacteria in root nodules of leguminous plants fix nitrogen, improving soil fertility. Free-living bacteria like *Azotobacter* and *Azospirillum* also fix atmospheric nitrogen. Mycorrhizal fungi, such as *Glomus,* form symbiotic relationships with plants, improving soil fertility by absorbing and transferring phosphorus, while also providing resistance to pathogens and tolerance to drought and salinity.

Cyanobacteria, like *Nostoc* and *Anabaena,* fix nitrogen in both aquatic and terrestrial environments, particularly in paddy fields, and contribute organic matter to the soil.

Exercises

Question 1 Bacteria cannot be seen with the naked eyes, but these can be seen with the help of a microscope. If you have to carry a sample from your home to your biology laboratory to demonstrate the presence of microbes under a microscope, which sample would you carry and why?

Sol. A sample of curd could be opted for demonstrating the presence of microbes under a microscope as it would contain numerous lactic acid bacteria in it.

Question 2 Give examples to prove that microbes release gases during metabolism.

Sol. Examples to prove that microbes release gases during metabolism are as follow

(a) The puffed-up appearance of dough of dosa and idli is because of the CO_2 released by bacteria during fermentation of the dough.

(b) In waste water treatment, during the digestion of sludge bacteria produce a mixture of gases such as methane, hydrogen sulphide and carbon dioxide. These gases form biogas.

Question 3 In which food would you find lactic acid bacteria? Mention some of their useful applications.

Sol. Generally, Lactic Acid Bacteria (LAB), are found in milk and its products.

Lactic Acid Bacteria (LAB), are a group of related bacteria that produce lactic acid from carbohydrate fermentation. They are generally used in making fermented milk products.

(i) They can grow in milk, breakdown lactose sugar in the milk and produce acids that coagulate and partially digest the milk proteins. They also add vitamin-B_{12} in milk thereby increasing its nutritional quality.

(ii) In our stomach too, the LAB play very beneficial role in checking disease causing microbes.

Question 4 Name some traditional Indian foods made of wheat, rice and Bengal gram (or their products) which involve use of microbes.

Sol. For making dosa and idli, rice powder is fermented by bacteria and for making bread from wheat, yeast (*Saccharomyces cerevisiae*) is used. Gutta made from black gram (a type of bengal gram) is also fermented using bacteria.

Microbes are also used to ferment fish, soyabean and bamboo shoots to make foods.

Question 5 In which way have microbes played a major role in controlling diseases caused by harmful bacteria?

Sol. Microbes produce certain chemical substances, called antibiotics that can be used to kill or retard the growth of other disease causing microbes.

These antibiotics are used to treat deadly diseases such as plague, whooping cough (kali khansi), diphtheria (galghotu) and leprosy (kusht rog) and many other common infections. *e.g.* streptomycin, erythromycin.

Penicillin was the first antibiotic to be discovered from fungus *Penicillium notatum.*

Question 6 Name any two species of fungus, which are used in the production of the antibiotics.

Sol. *Penicillium notatum* and *Aspergillus fumigatus* are two species of fungus, which are used in the production of the antibiotics.

Question 7 What is sewage? In which way can sewage be harmful to us?

Sol. Sewage is the municipal waste-water collected from city or town homes, that contains toilet, bathroom and kitchen waste.

It contains large amounts of organic matter and many pathogenic microbes which are harmful to humans as they can cause many diseases like cholera, typhoid, dysentery etc. Therefore, it must be discharged into the natural water bodies only after proper treatment.

Question 8 What is the key difference between primary and secondary sewage treatment?

Sol. Primary treatment involves physical removal of large and small particles from the sewage throught filtration and sedimentation.

Whereas, secondary sewage treatment involves biological digestion of organic matter by microbes.

Question 9 Do you think microbes can also be used as source of energy? If yes, how?

Sol. Microbes can be used as a source of energy as certain bacteria like, *Methanobacterium,* can generate biogas.

Cow dung can be used for the production of biogas as it is rich in *Methonobacterium.*

Biogas is a mixture of gases such as methane, hydrogen sulphide and carbon dioxide. This gas is inflammable and can be used as a fuel.

The biogas plant has a concrete tank about 10-15 feet deep. In it the biowastes are collected and a slurry of dung is fed. The plant has an outlet pipe through which the biogas reaches to nearby houses.

Then, it is used for cooking and lighting.

Question 10 Microbes can be used to decrease the use of chemical fertilisers and pesticides. Explain how this can be accomplished.

Sol. Microbes can be used as biofertilisers, (organisms that enrich the nutrient quality of the soil) and biopesticides (organisms/agents used to control pests)

The main sources of bio-fertilisers are bacteria, fungi and cyanobacteria.

They help in increasing the fertility of the soil in many ways

 (i) *Rhizobium* that forms nodules on the roots of leguminous plants (a symbiotic association) fixes atmospheric nitrogen into organic forms, which is used by the plant as nutrient.

 (ii) *Azospirillum* and *Azotobacter* fix atmospheric nitrogen, while living freely, and enriching the nitrogen content of the soil.

 (iii) Many members of the genus *Glomus* (fungi) form symbiotic associations with plant known as mycorrhiza that absorb phosphorus from soil and pass it to the plant and help the plants to develop resistance to root-borne pathogens increase their tolerance to salinity and drought and thus, help in overall increase in plant growth and development.

 (iv) *Cyanobacteria* are autotrophic microbes, such as *Anabaena, Nostoc, Oscillatoria* can fix atmospheric nitrogen, in aquatic and terrestrial environment and also add organic matter to the soil and increase its fertility.

 Microbes can be used as biopesticides to control insect pests in plants, e.g., *Bacillus thuringiensis* which produces toxins to kill the pest. Another organism is Baculovirus which is a pathogen that attack insects.

Question 11 Three water samples namely river water, untreated sewage water and secondary effluent discharged from a sewage treatment plant were subjected to BOD test. The samples were labelled A, B and C; but the laboratory attendant did not note which was which. The BOD values of the three samples A, B and C were recorded as 20 mg/L, 8 mg/L and 400 mg/L, respectively. Which sample of the water is most polluted?
Can you assign the correct label to each assuming the river water is relatively clean?

Sol. Sample A (BOD 20mg/L) is secondary effluent discharged from a sewage treatment plant.
Sample B (BOD 8mg/L) is river water.
Sample C (BOD 400mg/L) is the untreated sewage water.
As BOD is the direct measure of the organic matter present in water, higher the BOD, more polluted the water. The most polluted sample is sample C

Question 12 Find out the name of the microbes from which Cyclosporin-A (an immunosuppressive drug) and statins (blood cholesterol lowering agents) are obtained.

Sol.   (i) Cyclosporin-A is obtained from the fungus *Trichoderma polysporum*.

(ii) Statins is obtained from *Monascus purpureus*.

Question 13 Find out the role of microbes in the following and discuss it with your teacher.

(a) Single Cell Protein (SCP)

(b) Soil

Sol.   (a) Single Cell Protein (SCP) refers to harmless microbial cells that can be used as an alternate source of good protein.

Microbes like *Spirulina* and *Methylophilus methylotrophus* are being grown on an industrial scale. These single cell microbes can be used as source of proteins as SCP has a range of uses

(i) Animal feed (ii) Dietary supplement for humans, (iii) As a substitute for meat (iv) As a food ingredient.

(b) Role of microbes in soil. Soil contains both harmful and useful microbes which play an important role in it.

Some bacteria help fix atmospheric nitrogen into organic forms which plants can use as nutrient.

(i) *Rhizobium* that forms nodules on the roots of leguminous plants (a symbiotic association) fixes atmospheric nitrogen into organic forms, which is used by the plant as nutrient.

(ii) *Azospirillum* and *Azotobacter* fix atmospheric nitrogen, while living freely, and enriching the nitrogen content of the soil.

(iii) Many members of the genus Glomus (fungi) form symbiotic associations with plant known as mycorrhiza that absorb phosphorus from soil and pass it to the plant.

(iv) Cyanobacteria autotrophic microbes, *e.g.*, *Anabaena, Nostoc, Oscillatoria* can fix atmospheric nitrogen, in aquatic and terrestrial environment and also add organic matter to the soil and increase its fertility. (Mineralisation)

(v) Organic remains of plants and animals fall over the soil. Microbes partially degrade the matter and convert it into humans. (Humification)

Question 14 Arrange the following in the decreasing order (most important first) of their importance, for the welfare of human society. Give reasons for your answer.

Biogas, Citric acid, Penicillin, Curd.

Sol. **Penicillin** is an antibiotic that helps kill pathogens that cause infections and diseases and thus, saves lives.

Biogas is a non-polluting clean fuel that is produced as a by product of sewage treatment. It is used for cooking and lighting up the homes in rural areas. The over slurry can be used as a manure to imporve soil ferticity.

Curd is obtained by the action of *Lactobacillus* bacteria on milk. It is a milk product which is found commonly in households.

Citric acid it is used as preservative of food and hence is the least important.

Question 15 How do biofertilisers enrich the fertility of the soil?

Sol. Biofertilisers are organisms that enrich the nutrient quality of soil. They enrich the soil by the use of various organisms. Many species of bacteria and cyanobacteria have the ability to fix free atmospheric nitrogen into organic forms that plants can use as nutrient.

For example,

(1) *Rhizobium* is a symbiotic bacterium that is found in the root nodules of leguminous plants where as *Azospirillium* and *Azotobacter* are free-living and fix atmospheric nitrogen.

(2) *Anabaena, Nostoc* and *Oscillatoria* are cyanobacteria that fix atmospheric nitrogen.

DIKSHA APP *Questions*

Q.1 Which is an incorrect statement about 'LAB'?

(a) It is a group of bacteria that produce acid
(b) A group of bacteria that helps in coagulation of milk
(c) Helps in formation of curd
(d) They completely digest the milk proteins

Sol. (d) LAB partially digests milk protein by breaking down lactose into lactic acid and converting some milk proteins into peptides and amino acids.

Q.2 The large holes in 'Swiss cheese' are due to the:

(a) production of alcohol   (b) production of carbon dioxide
(c) production of oxygen   (d) process of distillation

Sol. (b) The large holes in Swiss cheese are due to the production of carbon dioxide gas by bacteria during fermentation.

Q.3 The 'Roquefort cheese' is ripened by growing a specific:

(a) Fungi   (b) Bacteria   (c) LAB   (d) Yeast

Sol. (a) Roquefort cheese is ripened by the growth of a specific fungus called *Penicillium roqueforti.*

Q.4 The alcoholic drinks produced without distillation is:

(a) brandy, wine   (b) beer, wine   (c) whisky, beer   (d) rum, brandy

Sol. (b) Wine and beer are alcoholic drink produced through fermentation without the process of distillation.

Q.5 The chemical substances produced by some microbes which can kill or retard the growth of other microbes are called:

(a) toddy   (b) antibodies   (c) antibiotics   (d) STPs

Sol. (c) Antibiotics are chemical substances produced by some microbes that can kill or inhibit the growth of other microbes.

Q.6 Which of the following organism is not used in the production of organic acid/alcohol?

(a) *Penicillium notatum*   (b) *Saccharomyces cerevisiae*
(c) *Aspergillus niger*   (d) *Clostridium butylicum*

Sol. (a) *Penicillium notatum* is used to produce an antibiotic (i.e. penicillin), not organic acids or alcohols.

Q.7 Alexander Fleming discovered penicillin while working on

(a) *Penicillum notatum*   (b) Staphylococci
(c) Bacillus   (d) Brown mold

Sol. (b) Alexander Fleming discovered penicillin while working on *Staphylococcus* bacteria.

Q.8 Which of the antibiotics was discovered first?

(a) Streptomycin   (b) Penicillin   (c) Neomycin   (d) Erythromycin

Sol. (b) Penicillin was the first antibiotic to be discovered by Alexander Fleming in 1928.

Q.9 Which of the following is not an acid producing bacterium?

(a) *Aspergillus niger* (b) *Streptococcus* (c) *Acetobacter*   (d) *Lactobacillus*

Sol. (a) *Aspergillus niger* is a fungus, not a bacterium, and is commonly used in the production of citric acid.

Q.10 An important bioactive molecule used as an imunosuppressant is:

(a) cyclosporin A (b) cyclosporin B
(c) cyclosporin D (d) cyclosporin E

Sol. (a) Cyclosporin A is an important bioactive molecule used as an immunosuppressant to prevent organ rejection in transplant patients.

Q.11 Which of the following bacteria has a role in removing clots in our blood vessels:

(a) *Bacillus thuringiensis* (b) *Clostridium butylicum*
(c) *Streptococcus* (d) *Lactobacillus*

Sol. (c) *Streptococcus* bacteria are used in medical applications to dissolve blood clots in blood vessels.

Q.12 Statins produced by the yeast *Monascus purpureus* have been commercialised as

(a) immunosppressants
(b) antibiotics
(c) blood cholesterol-lowering agents
(d) clot busters

Sol. (c) Statins are commercialised as blood cholesterol-lowering agents, used to reduce cholesterol levels and prevent cardiovascular diseases.

Q.13 Cyclosporin A is produced by

(a) *Streptococcus* (b) *Staphylococci*
(c) *Trichoderma polysporum* (d) *Bacillus thuringiensis*

Sol. (c) Cyclosporin A is produced by *Trichoderma polysporum*, a fungus.

Q.14 Which of the following is used as a biofertiliser?

(a) Cyanobacteria (b) Yeast
(c) Symbiotic bacteria (d) Free living bacteria

Sol. (a) Cyanobacteria can fix nitrogen in the soil, which helps control nitrogen deficiency in plants.

Q.15 The process of sequential filtration during primary treatment of sewage removes

(a) grit and stones (b) soil and pebbles
(c) floating debris (d) solids

Sol. (c) Sequential filtration during the primary treatment of sewage removes floating debris, such as leaves, plastic, and other large particles.

Q.16 .... is involved in primary treatment of sewage
- (a) aeration
- (b) sedimentation
- (c) mechanical agitation
- (d) reduction of BOD

Sol. (b) Sedimentation is involved in the primary treatment of sewage, where solid particles settle at the bottom of the tank, separating from the water.

Q.17 Sewage cannot be discharged into natural water bodies because:
- (a) It contains large amount of inorganic matter and aerobic microbes
- (b) It contains large amount of organic matter and pathogenic microbes
- (c) It contains large number of organic matter and useful microbes
- (d) It contains large number of acid releasing and aerobic microbes

Sol. (b) Sewage contains large amounts of organic matter and pathogenic microbes, making it harmful to aquatic life and public health.

Q.18 Methanogens are found in:
- (a) methanol
- (b) organic acid
- (c) anaerobic sludge
- (d) inorganic acid

Sol. (c) Methanogens are microorganisms that thrive in anaerobic conditions, such as in anaerobic sludge, where they produce methane as a byproduct of the decomposition of organic matter.

Q.19 The technology of Biogas production in india has been developed by the efforts of:
- (a) KVIC and IARI
- (b) ICAR
- (c) KVIC
- (d) ICMR

Sol. (a) The technology of biogas production in India has been developed through the efforts of KVIC (Khadi and Village Industries Commission) and IARI (Indian Agricultural Research Institute).

Biotechnology : Principles and Processes

CHAPTER 09

Important Points

01 Biotechnology in modern concept, refers to the processes which uses genetically modified organisms to make various commercial products on a large scale.

02 Principles of Biotechnology

The two core techniques of modern biotechnology are **genetic engineering** and **bioprocess engineering**.

03 Genetic engineering is a deliberate modification of an organism's DNA, using various techniques. This altered DNA (recombined DNA) is then introduced into the host organism to change its phenotype.

04 Stanley cohen and Herbert Boyer constructed the first recombinant DNA in 1972. They isolated the antibiotic resistant gene from plasmid of bacteria and then linked the gene with plasmid (of *Salmonella typhimurium*) and incoperated into *E coli*, where it could replicate using the host's DNA polymerase enzyme and make multiple copies.

05 Tools of Recombinant DNA Technology

The key tools required for recombinant technology are restriction enzymes, ligases, polymerase enzymes, vectors and host organism/cell

06 **Restriction Enzymes** (REs) are called molecular scissors and are responsible for cutting DNA. They serve as a key defence mechanism in bacteria against viral attack, as they cut the viral DNA into pieces thereby restricting the growth of invading bacteriophages.

(i) They cut the DNA at specific base sequences, known as **recognition sequences** and can be used to create recombinant DNA molecule.

(ii) The convention for naming these enzymes is the first letter of the name comes from the genus and the second two letters come from the species of the prokaryotic cell from which they were isolated.

Roman numbers following the names indicate the order in which the enzymes were isolated from that strain of bacteria.

Examples of REs

Restriction Enzyme	Isolated from	Recognition Sequence
Hind II	*Haemophilus influenza* Rd	5′ —G T C G A C—3′ 3′ —C A G C T G—5′
Eco RI	*Escherichia coli* RY 13	5′ —G A A T T C—3′ 3′ —C T T A A G—5′

(iii) Restriction enzymes are of two kinds—**exonucleases** (removes nucleotides from the outer ends of DNA) and **endonucleases** (make cuts at specific position within the DNA)

(iv) Each restriction endonuclease recognises a specific **palindromic nucleotide** sequences.

(v) Restriction enzymes cut the strand of DNA a little away from the center of the palindrome sites and thus creates sticky ends. These stickiness of the ends facilitates the action of the enzyme DNA ligase.

07 Separation of restriction fragments from each other on the basis of size can be done by **gel electrophoresis**.

- The separated DNA fragments are visualised after staining with ethidium bromide, followed by exposure to UV light.
- The DNA bands are then extracted from the gel through a process called elution. These purified fragments can be used to create DNA by ligating them into cloning vectors.

08 **Cloning Vectors** are DNA fragments that carry a foreign DNA segment into the host cells. Plasmids and bacteriophages have the ability to replicate within the bacterial cells independent of chromosomal DNA, so they are used as **cloning vectors**.

09 Features that are required to facilitate cloning into a vector are as follows.

(i) **Origin of replication** (*ori*)   This is a sequence from where replication starts and any piece of DNA when linked to this sequence can be made to replicate within the host cells.

(ii) **Selectable marker**   It helps in identifying and eliminating non-transformants and selectively permitting the growth of the transformants.

(iii) **Cloning sites** These are specific DNA sequences within a vector that are recognised by restriction enzymes and allow the insertion of foreign DNA for cloning.

pBR322 is one of the most widely used artificial cloning vector.

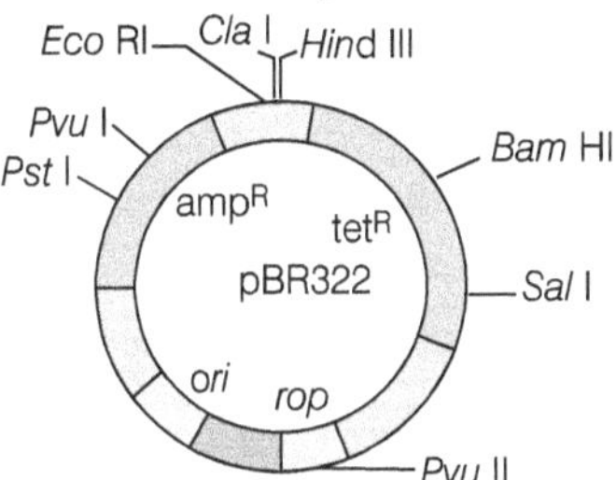

▲ *E. coli* cloning vector pBR322

10 Competent Host

- DNA cannot pass through cell membranes due to its hydrophilic nature, so bacteria are made 'competent' to take up plasmid DNA by treating them with calcium and applying heat shock.
- Other methods of DNA introduction include microinjection, gene guns and disarmed pathogen vectors.

11 Processes of Recombinant DNA Technology

The recombinant DNA technology involves several steps in a specific sequence which are as follows

(i) **Isolation of Genetic Material** (DNA) It can be achieved by treating cells with enzymes like lysozyme (bacterial), cellulase (plant cells) or chitinase (fungus) to break them open, releasing DNA with other macromolecules.

RNA and proteins are removed with ribonuclease and protease respectively and then purified DNA is precipitated by adding chilled ethanol.

(ii) **Cutting of DNA at Specific Locations**

(i) It is done using restriction enzymes followed by agarose gel electrophoresis to check the progress of restriction enzyme digestion.

(iii) The cut out **gene of interest** from the source DNA and the **vector** with a cut space are mixed followed by addition of ligase resulting in the formation of recombinant DNA.

(iii) **Amplification of Gene of Interest using PCR**

PCR stands for **Polymerase Chain Reaction,** a method of amplifying fragments of DNA. This method can make multiple copies of even a single DNA fragment or the gene of interest, in vitro using primers and thermostable DNA polymerase (Taq polymerase)

The amplified fragment can be used to ligate with a vector for further cloning.

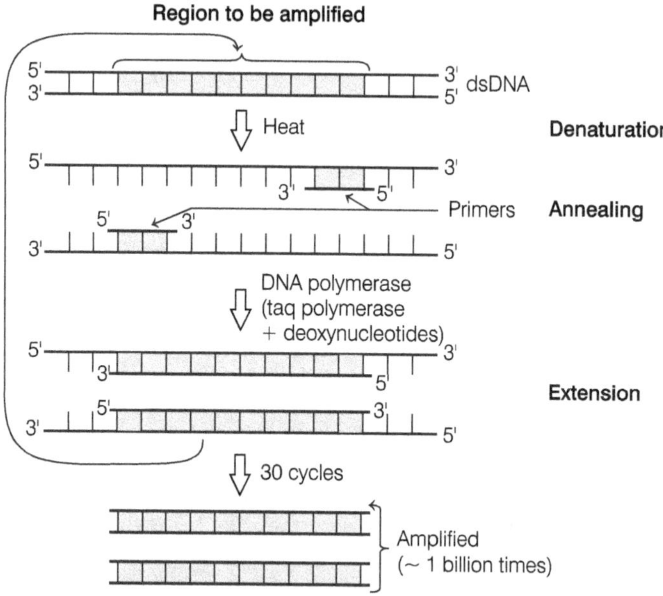

▲ Polymerase Chain Reaction (PCR) : Each cycle has three steps
(i) Denaturation (ii) Prime annealing (iii) Extension of primers

(iv) **Insertion of Recombinant DNA into the Host Cell/Organism** Introduction of ligated DNA into the recipient cell occurs by several methods, before which the recipient cells are made competent to receive the DNA

   (i) If a recombinant DNA bearing antibiotic resistance gene (*e.g.*, ampicillin) is transferred into *E. coli* cells, the host cells become transformed into ampicillin-resistant cells.

   (ii) On growing the transformed cells on agar plates containing ampicillin, only transformants will grow and others will die.

(v) **Obtaining the Foreign Gene Product**
   - When a protein encoding gene is expressed in a heterologous host, it is called a **recombinant protein**.
   - The cells harbouring cloned genes of interest may be grown on a small scale in the laboratory or on a large scale using bioreactors.
   - Bioreactors are large vessels (100-1000 L capacity) in which raw materials are biologically converted into specific products, individual enzymes, etc., using microbial, plant, animal or human cells.
   - It is specially designed to provide the optimal conditions of temperature, pH, substrate, salts, vitamins, oxygen, etc., for achieving the desired production levels.

(vi) **Downstream Processing** All the processes to which a product is subjected to before being marketed as a finished product are called downstream processing.

   It includes separation and purification of product, formulation with suitable preservatives and quality control testing.

Exercises

Question 1 Can you list 10 recombinant proteins which are used in medical practice? Find out where they are used as therapeutics (use the internet).

Sol.

S.N.	Recombinant Protein	Use
1.	Human insulin	Treatment of diabetes mellitus
2.	Blood clotting factor VII	Treatment of haemophilia-A
3.	Blood clotting factor IX	Treatment of haemophilia-B
4.	Hepatitis-B vaccine	Prevention of hepatitis-B
5.	Inter leukins	To enhance the activity of immune system.
6.	Platelet growth factor	Stimulation of wound healing
7.	Hirudin	As anticoagulant
8.	Tissue plasminogen activator	To dissolves blood clots in acute myocardial infarction
9.	Asparaginase	Treatment of blood cancer
10.	ReoPro	Prevention of blood clots

Question 2 Make a chart (with diagrammatic representation) showing a restriction enzyme, the substrate DNA on which it acts, the site at which it cuts DNA and the product it produces.

Note Solution 2 given on next page

Sol. The diagrammatic representation of action of restriction enzyme, *ECORI* is as follows:

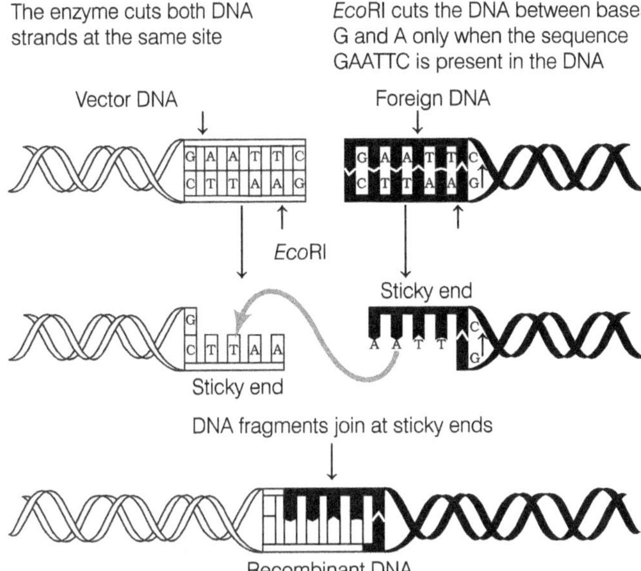

Steps in formation of recombinant DNA by action of restriction endonuclease enzyme (*Eco* RI)

Question 3 From what you have learnt, can you tell whether enzymes are bigger or DNA is bigger in molecular size? How did you know?

Sol. DNA is bigger in molecular size than enzymes. Because DNA is a long double stranded molecule which can go up to a few meters in length, when stretched end to end but enzymes although variable in size, would still be smaller than the DNA.

Question 4 What would be the molar concentration of human DNA in a human cell? Consult your teacher.

Sol. Total mass of DNA in a cell $= 6 \times 10^{-12}\,g$

Molecular weight of one base pair $= 650\,Da$

no. of base pairs $= 3 \times 10^{9}$

Volume of human cell $= 1 \times 10^{-12}\,L$

Molar mass $= 3 \times 10^{9} \times 650\,Da = 1.95 \times 10^{12}\,Da$

$$\text{Moles of DNA in one cell} = \frac{\text{Total mass of DNA}}{\text{Molecular mass}} = \frac{6 \times 10^{-12}}{1.95 \times 10^{12}}$$

$$= 3.08 \times 10^{-24} \text{ mol}$$

$$\text{Molar concentration} = \frac{3.08 \times 10^{-24} \text{ mol}}{1 \times 10^{-12} \text{ L}} = 3.08 \times 10^{-12} \text{ m}$$

Question 5 Do eukaryotic cells have restriction endonucleases? Justify your answer.

Sol. No, eukaryotic cells do not have restriction endonucleases.

This is because the restriction endonucleases serves as defense mechanism in prokaryotes (bacteria) to destroy the foreign DNA, if it invades the cell. It is generally prokaryotes that get infected by naked viral and foreign DNA that needs to be destroyed. Moreover, DNA of eukaryotes is highly methylated by a modification of enzyme, called methylase, methylation protects the DNA from the activity of restriction enzymes.

Question 6 Besides better aeration and mixing properties, what other advantages do stirred tank bioreactors have over shake flasks?

Sol. Stirred tank bioreactor are developed for the large scale production of biotechnology products where as the shake flasks are used for small scale production of biotechnological products carried out in a laboratory. Besides better aeration and mixing properties, stirred tank bioreactors have many advantages over shake flasks which are as follows.

  (i) They have a foam control and oxygen delivery system.

 (ii) They have a temperature and pH control system.

(iii) They have sampling ports so that small volumes of the culture can be withdrawn periodically.

Question 7 Collect five examples of palindromic DNA sequences by consulting your teacher.

Better try to create a palindromic sequence by following base-pair rules.

Sol.   (i) 5′ −A A G C T T−3′
             3′ −T T C G A A−5′

  (ii) 5′ −G A A T T C−3′
             3′ −C T T A A G−5′

(iii) 5′ −A C T A G T−3′
             3′ −T G A T C A−5′

 (iv) 5′ −G T C G A C−3′
             3′ −C A G C T G−5′

  (v) 5′ −G G A T C C−3′
             3′ −C C T A G G−5′

Question 8 Can you recall meiosis and indicate at what stage a recombinant DNA is made?

Sol. Recombinant DNA is made during pachytene stage of prophase-I of meiosis-I. It is formed due to crossing over between non-sister chromatids of homologous chromosomes.

Question 9 Can you think and answer how a reporter enzyme can be used to monitor transformation of host cells by foreign DNA in addition to a selectable marker?

Sol. A reporter enzyme can be used to monitor transformation of host cells by keeping a track of its reporter gene. Examples of reporter enzymes include β-galactosidase or alkaline phosphatase. They have particular characteristics that allow visual or spectrophotometric detection of the activity of their coresponding genes. If host cells are transformed by the uptake of foreign DNA, that will cause insertional inactivation of the enzyme gene β-galactosidase the gene product will not express and colonies of host cells will appear colourless in the presence of a chromogenic substrate, whereas non-transformed cells will make blue coloured colonies as their enzyme will be active.

Question 10 Describe briefly the following

   (a) Origin of replication

   (b) Bioreactors

   (c) Downstream processing

Sol. (a) **Origin of replication** (*ori*) is a sequence on the chromosome, from where replication starts and any piece of DNA when linked to this sequence can be made to replicate within the host cells. This sequence also controls the copy number of the linked DNA. In order to recover many copies of the target DNA it should be linked to the '*ori*' site and should be cloned in a vector whose origin supports high copy number.

   (b) **Bioreactors** are large vessels in which raw materials are biologically converted into specific products, individual enzymes, etc., using microbial, plant, animal or human cells.

   A bioreactor provides the optimal conditions for achieving the desired products providing optimum growth conditions i.e, temperature, pH, substrate, salts, vitamins, oxygen, etc.

   (c) **Downstream processing** includes the method of separation and purification, of foreign gene products after the completion of the biosynthetic phase.

   The product has to be formulated with suitable preservatives. Such formulation has to undergo clinical trials as in case of drugs.

   Strict quality control testing for each product is also required. The downstream processing and quality control testing vary from product to product.

Question 11 Explain briefly

(a) PCR

(b) Restriction enzymes and DNA

(c) Chitinase

Sol. PCR stands for polymerase chain reaction. It is a technique through which several copies of a certain DNA segment can be made.

The PCR technique uses two sets of primers and the enzyme DNA polymerase. The enzymes extends the primers using nucleotides in the reaction and using the genomic DNA as template.

The PCR cycle involves three major steps.

(1) **Denaturation** In this step, double stranded DNA is converted into single stranded by heating at high temperature.

(2) **Annealing** The two sets of primers undergo biochemical process of annealing

(3) **Extension** The enzyme DNA polymerase extends these primers. When the process of replication is repeated many times, the segment of DNA can be amplified to make a billion copies of it.

(b) **Restriction enzymes** are used in genetic engineering to cut the large DNA molecule into smaller fragments.

They are also known as molecular scissors. These are of two types: endonuclease and exonuclease. Exonucleases removes nucleotides from the ends of DNA whereas, endonucleases make cut at specific position within the DNA.

When DNA from two different sources are cut by the same restriction enzyme (endonuclease) the resultant DNA fragments have the same kind of 'sticky-ends' and these can be joined together (end-to-end) using DNA ligases.

This new DNA created by joining fragments, from two different sources / genomes together, is called recombinant DNA.

(c) **Chitinase** is an enzyme that breaks down chitin, a component of fungal cell wall. It is useful for isolating the fungal cell DNA.

Question 12   Discuss with your teacher and find out how to distinguish between

(a) Plasmid DNA and chromosomal DNA?

(b) RNA and DNA?

(c) Exonuclease and endonuclease?

Sol.

(a)

S.N.	Plasmid DNA	Chromosomal DNA
1.	It is a circular extra chromosomal DNA.	It is generally linear.
2.	It is not associated with histone proteins.	It is associated with histone proteins.
3	It contains very few genes which may not be necessary for the cell.	It is consists of complete genome vital for the cellular functions.
4.	It is used as a vector.	It is not used as a vector.

(b)

S.N.	DNA	RNA
1.	It is double stranded nucleic acid.	It single stranded nucleic acids.
2.	It has deoxyribose sugar component.	It has ribose sugar component.
3.	It has four nucleotides that act as its building blocks-adenine, guanine, cytosine and thymine.	Along with adenine, guanine and cytosine, It has uracil instead of thymine.
4.	It can replicate on it own	It can not replicate on it own
5.	It is generally present in the nucleus of the cell and some organelle.	It is present in both nucleus and cytoplasm.

(c)

S.N.	Exonucleases	Endonucleases
1.	They remove nucleotides from the outer ends of the DNA.	They make cuts at specific regions within the DNA
2.	They act on the single strand of DNA.	They act on either one or both the strands of DNA.

DIKSHA APP Questions

☐ Multiple Choice Questions

Q.1 Restriction enzymes belong to a larger class of enzymes called
    (a) Nucleases   (b) Ligases
    (c) Isomerases   (d) Transferases

Sol. (a) Restriction enzymes belong to a larger class of enzymes called nucleases, which are responsible for cutting DNA at specific sequences.

Q.2 Which specific DNA sequences responsible for initiating replication?
    (a) palindromic sequence   (b) recognitions sequence
    (c) origin of replication   (d) selectable marker

Sol. (c) The origin of replication is the specific DNA sequence where the replication process begins, serving as the site where helicase unwinds the DNA to initiate copying.

Q.3 Select the cloning vectors from the following:
    (a) Bacteriophage and fungi   (b) Fungi and bacteria
    (c) Bacteriophage and plasmid   (d) Plasmid and bacteria

Sol. (c) Bacteriophages and plasmids are commonly used as cloning vectors to transfer foreign DNA into host cells for replication and expression.

Q.4 Name the bacterium which produces tumors in dicot plants.
    (a) *Agrobacterium tumefaciens*   (b) *Bacillus thuringiensis*
    (c) *Acetobacter aceti*   (d) *Streptococcus*

Sol. (a) *Agrobacterium tumefaciens* is a bacterium that causes tumors, known as crown gall disease, in dicot plants by transferring a segment of its DNA into the plant's genome.

Q.5 Name the process through which a piece of DNA is introduced to a host bacterium
    (a) translation   (b) electrophoresis
    (c) transformation   (d) insertional inactivation

Sol. (c) Transformation is the process through which a piece of DNA is introduced into a host bacterium, allowing the bacterium to take up and incorporate foreign genetic material.

Q.6 Which of the following is not used for introduction of alien DNA into host cells?

(a) Micro injection   (b) Elution

(c) Gene gun   (d) Competent bacteria

Sol. (b) Elution is the process of extracting a substance from a mixture by washing it with a solvent.

Q.7 Which enzyme produced by *Thermus aquaticus* is used for amplification of genes using PCR?

(a) RNA polymerase   (b) DNA ligase

(c) *Taq* polymerase   (d) Endonuclease

Sol. (c) *Taq* polymerase, an enzyme produced by *Thermus aquaticus,* is used for the amplification of genes in PCR (Polymerase Chain Reaction) due to its ability to withstand high temperatures.

Q.8 What are the optimal conditions provided by a bioreactor?

(a) Substrate, CO_2, pH, salts, temperature & vitamins.

(b) Temperature, enzymes, pH, salts, vitamins & CO_2.

(c) Temperature, enzymes, pH, salts, vitamins & O_2.

(d) Temperature, pH, substrate, salts, vitamins & O_2.

Sol. (d) A bioreactor provides optimal conditions such as controlled temperature, pH, substrates, salts, vitamins, and oxygen to support the growth and metabolic activity of microorganisms or cells for efficient production.

☐ Short Answer Type

Q.1 Name the scientists who constructed the first recombinant DNA. How?

Sol. The first recombinant DNA molecules were constructed by Herbert Boyer, and Stanley Cohen in 1972. They isolate the antibiotic resistance gene by cutting out a piece of DNA from a plasmid. Which was responsible for conferring antibiotic resistance with the help to restriction enzyme. The cut piece of DNA was then linked with the vector DNA with the help of enzyme DNA ligase.

Q.2 State the steps involved in the Recombinant DNA technology.

Sol. Steps involved in the recombinant DNA technology are as follows-:
1. Isolation of Genetic Material
2. Cutting of DNA at specific locations using restriction endonuclases.
3. Amplification of gene of interest using PCR.
4. Ligation of DNA Molecules in to a vector.
5. Insertion of Recombinant DNA Into Host.
6. Obtaining Foreign Gene Product.
7. Downstream Processing.

Q.3 Explain the process of separation and isolation of DNA fragment

Sol. DNA fragments are produced by cutting DNA with restriction endonucleases, and these fragments can be separated using gel electrophoresis. Since DNA fragments are negatively charged, they move towards the anode under an electric field through a matrix, typically agarose gel, a natural polymer derived from seaweed. The gel acts as a sieve, allowing DNA fragments to separate based on size-the smaller fragments travel farther than larger ones.

After electrophoresis, the DNA fragments. are visualized by staining with ethidium bromide and exposing the gel to UV light. The stained DNA appears as bright orange bands-under UV light. These bands can be cut out from the gel and extracted through a process called elution.

Biotechnology and Its Applications

CHAPTER 10

Important Points

01 Biotechnology deals with the industrial scale production of biopharmaceuticals and biologicals using genetically modified microbes, fungi, plants and animals.

02 Biotechnology has made available to humans several useful products by using microbes, plant, animals and their metabolic machinery.

03 The applications of biotechnology include therapeutics, diagnostics, GM crops, processed foods, bioremediation, waste treat and energy production.

04 Three critical areas of research in biotechnology are

   (i) providing the best catalyst in the form of improved organism (a microbe) or pure enzyme.

   (ii) creating optimal conditions (through engineering) for the catalyst to act.

   (iii) downstream processing technologies to purify the protein/ organic compound.

05 Biotechnological Applications in Agriculture

The three ways for increasing food production are agro-chemical based agriculture, organic agriculture, genetically engineered crop-based agriculture.

06 The **green revolution** succeeded in increasing crop yields due to the use of improved crop varieties, better crop management practices and agrochemicals (fertilisers and pesticides). However, agrochemicals are costly for many farmers and conventional breeding cannot further increases yields.

07 Tissue culture involves growing plants from explants in sterile nutrient media, enabling rapid propagation of plants. The ability to regenerate a whole plant from any cell or explant is called **totipotency.** Plants produced through this method are genetically identical to the original plant and are called **somaclones.** This technique is widely used for crops like tomato, banana, and apple.

Tissue culture is used to recover virus-free plants by culturing the virus free meristems of infected plants, as done with banana, sugarcane, and potato. In somatic hybridisation, protoplasts from different plants are fused to create somatic hybrids, such as the experimental pomato, combining traits of tomato and potato.

08 Plants, bacteria, fungi and animals whose genes have been altered by manipulation are called **Genetically Modified Organisms** (GMOs).

GM plants show following characterstics.

  (i) They are more tolerant to abiotic stresses (cold, drought, salt and heat).

  (ii) They reduced reliance on chemical pesticides (pest-resistant crops).

  (iii) They increased efficiency of mineral usage prevents early exhaustion of fertility of soil.

  (iv) They enhanced the nutritional value of food, *e.g.* Vitamin-A enriched rice.

09 **Insect Resistant Transgenic Plants** Biotechnology in agriculture includes creating pest-resistant plants like *Bt* cotton and *Bt* corn. These plants carry the *Bt* toxin gene from *Bacillus thuringiensis*, making them insect-resistant without using insecticides.

10 **Mode of Action of *Bt* Toxin** Bt cotton contains a gene from *Bacillus thuringiensis* (*Bt*) that produces an insecticidal protein. The protein is initially inactive but becomes active in the insect's alkaline gut, where it forms pores in gut cells, leading to the insect's death. Different *Bt* toxin genes, such as cryllAc and cryllAb, target specific pests like cotton bollworms and corn borers.

11 Pest Resistant Transgenic Plants Pest-resistant plants can be created using RNA interference (RNAi) to protect against nematodes like *Meloidoqyne incognitia,* which infect tobacco roots. By introducing nematode-specific genes into plants via Agrobacterium vectors, both sense and anti-sense RNA are produced, forming double-stranded RNA (*ds*RNA). This triggers RNAi, silencing the nematode's mRNA, preventing the parasite from surviving in the transgenic plant.

12 Biotechnological Applications in Medicine Recombinant DNA technology has greatly impacted healthcare by enabling the mass production of safe, effective therapeutic drugs that avoid immunological responses typical of non-human sources. Currently, around 30 recombinant therapeutics are approved worldwide, with 12 available in India.

13 Vaccines The techniques of modern biotechnology such as genetical engineering and oil culture enable and effective quick and economical development of vaccines.

14 Genetically Engineered Insulin Insulin was previously extracted from the pancreas of cattle and pigs, but it often caused allergies or other reactions due to the foreign protein. Insulin consists of two polypeptide chains, A and B, linked by disulfide bridges. In humans, insulin is produced as a prohormone with an extra C peptide, which is removed in mature insulin.

The challenge in *r*DNA based production was assembling mature insulin. In 1983, *Eli Lilly* created DNA sequences for the A and B chains of human insulin and inserted them into *E. coli* plasmids. The chains were produced separately, extracted, and combined by forming disulfide bonds to create human insulin.

15 Gene Therapy Gene therapy involves correcting a genetic defect by inserting a normal gene into a person's cells or tissues. The first clinical gene therapy was performed in 1990 on a 4-year-old girl with adenosine deaminase (ADA) deficiency, a disorder affecting the immune system.

In this treatment, lymphocytes were cultured, and a functional ADA gene was introduced, then returned to the patient. Enzyme replacement therapy or bone marrow transplant can also treat ADA deficiency. Introducing the gene at early embryonic stages could offer a permanent cure.

16 Molecular Diagnosis Conventional methods like serum or urine analysis are not effective for early detection of pathogens or viruses. However, methods such as recombinant DNA technology, polymerase Chain Reaction (PCR), and Enzyme Linked Immuno-Sorbent Assay (ELISA) can diagnose diseases earlier.

PCR amplifies nucleic acids to detect low concentrations of pathogens, mutations in cancer genes, and genetic disorders, and is commonly used for HIV detection. ELISA detects infections by identifying antigens or antibodies against pathogens. Additionally, a technique involving hybridisation of radioactive DNA can help identify mutated genes in cells.

17 Transgenic Animals Transgenic animals, such as mice, rats, rabbits, pigs, sheep, cows, and fish, have been genetically modified to express foreign genes. They are developed for various purposes:

- **Gene Regulation and Physiology** To study gene function and its effect on normal body processes.
- **Disease Research** To understand how genes contribute to diseases like cancer, cystic fibrosis, and Alzheimer's.
- **Biological Products** To produce human proteins, such as alpha-1-antitrypsin, for medical use. For example, the transgenic cow rosie produced human protein-enriched milk.
- **Vaccine Safety** To test vaccine safety, such as the polio vaccine, on transgenic mice before human trials.
- **Chemical safety testing** Transgenic animals can be engineered to be more sensitive to toxic substances, allowing for faster chemical safety testing.

18 Ethical Issues Regarding Genetic Modification The Indian government established the GEAC to oversee GM research and safety. Biopatents grant exclusive rights for biological inventions, while biopiracy refers to unauthorised use of bio-resources by companies without compensation.

Exercises

Question 1 Which part of the plant is best suited for making virus-free plants and why?

Sol. Apical and axillary meristems are the parts, which are best suited for making virus-free plants because rate of division of meristematic cell is higher than rate of multiplication of virus, i.e. viruses are unable to invade newly formed meristematic cells.

Question 2 What is the major advantage of producing plants by micropropagation?

Sol. Micropropagation is the method by which thousand of plants are produced through tissue culture. These plants are genetically identical to the original plant and called as somclones.

Question 3 Find out what the various components of the medium used for propagation of an explant *in vitro* are?

Sol. Culture medium is used for the propagation of an explant. It contains nutrients like inorganic salts, vitamins, sucrose, amino-acid glycine and growth regulators like auxin and cytokinin. The culture medium can be kept liquid, made semisolid with gelatin or solidified with agar.

Question 4 Crystals of *Bt* toxin produced by some bacteria do not kill the bacteria themselves because

    (a) bacteria are resistant to the toxin
    (b) toxin is immature
    (c) toxin is inactive
    (d) bacteria encloses toxin in a special sac

Sol. (c) Crystals of *Bt* toxin produced by some bacteria do not kill the bacteria themselves because the toxin is present in inactive form (protoxin) inside the protein crystals produced by *B. thuringiensis* during a particular phase of its growth.

Question 5 What are transgenic bacteria? Illustrate using any one example.

Sol. Transgenic bacteria are modified bacteria, which carries a foreign gene and is used for the production of desired gene product.

    Example *E. coli* bacteria were genetically modified to carry the human insulin gene. These transgenic bacteria then produced insulin

Question 6 Compare and contrast the advantages and disadvantages of production of genetically modified crops.

Sol.   The advantages of GM crops are

  (i)   more tolerance to abiotic stresses (cold, drought, salt and heat).

  (ii) reduced reliance on chemical pesticides (pest-resistant crops).

  (iii) increased efficiency of mineral usage prevents early exhaustion of fertility of soil.

  (iv) enhanced nutritional value of food, *e.g.*, vitamin-A enriched rice.

In addition to these uses, GM has been used to create special plants to supply alternative resources to industries, in the form of starches, fuels and pharmaceuticals.

Disadvantages of such crops are

  (a)   transgenic genes in genetically modified crops endanger native species.

  (b)   they cause damage to natural environment by reducing biodiversity.

  (c)   they may cause human health problems by altered genes and transferred antibiotic resistance.

Question 7 What are *Cry* proteins? Name an organism that produce it. How has a man exploited this protein to his benefit?

Sol.   The proteins encoded by the gene named *Cry* are called *Cry* proteins. *Bt* toxin is the protein encoded by the gene *Cry*.

Organism that produces *Cry* proteins–*Bacillus thuringiensis*.

The *Cry* genes are incorporated in several crop plants, which then develop resistance to a specific targeted pest.

Example *CryIAc* and *CryIIAb* control the cotton bollworms, that of *Cry IAb* controls corn borer.

Question 8 What is gene therapy? Illustrate using the example of adenosine deaminase (ADA) deficiency.

Sol.   Gene therapy is a replacement of a defective or absent gene with a normal healthy gene, to correct a genetic disorder. Adenosine deaminase (ADA) deficiency is caused due to the deletion of gene, coding this enzyme.

To correct this disorder

  (i)   lymphocytes are isolated from the blood or bone marrow of the patient and grown in a culture outside the body.

  (ii) a functional ADA gene is then introduced into these lymphocytes, which are subsequently returned to the patient.

  (iii) since, these cells have a limited life, the patient requires repeated infusion of such genetically engineered lymphocytes.

  (iv) however, if the gene isolate from bone marrow cells producing ADA is introduced into cells at early embryonic stages, it could be a permanent cure.

Question 9 Digrammatically represent the experimental steps in cloning and expressing an human gene (say the gene for growth hormone) into a bacterium like *E. coli*?

Sol.

Diagrammatic representation of recombinant DNA technology

Question 10 Can you suggest a method to remove oil (hydrocarbon) from seeds based on your understanding of *r*DNA technology and chemistry of oil?

Sol. Oils are composed of glycerol and fatty acids. To remove oil from seeds using recombinant DNA technology would involve

   (i) identify the genes that code for glycerol or fatty acids.

   (ii) inserted the complementary gene sequence of these genes in the early cells of the endosperm.

   (iii) during the process of transcription these sequences will produce anti-sense RNA to the RNA produce by glycerol or fatty acids and will silence these genes.

Question 11 Find out from internet what is golden rice?

Sol. Golden rice is a new type of rice that contains large amount of beta carotene, a source of vitamin-A.

Golden rice was created by transforming the original rice with two β-carotene biosynthesis genes.

(i) *psy* (phytoene synthase) from daffodil (*Narcissus pseudonarcissus*).

(ii) *crt* I from the soil bacterium *Erwinia uredovora*.

These two genes together produce β-carotene in the rice grain.

Use of this rice can help reduce vitamin-A deficiency.

Question 12 Does our blood have proteases and nucleases?

Sol. Human blood does not have nucleases. But a variety of serine proteases (thrombin, plasmin, Hageman factor) are present in blood serum that plays an important role in blood-clotting, as well as in lysis of the clots.

Some other proteases (elastase and cathepsin G) are present in leukocytes and have several different roles in metabolic control. They also facilitate proper action of the immune system.

Question 13 Consult internet and find out how to make orally active protein pharmaceutical. What is the major problem to be encountered?

Sol. To make orally active protein pharmaceutical. It must be coated by a film or substance that is resistant to protein degrading enzymes. The major problem here is that the proteins with a short half lives are not orally active and are not absorbed properly.

DIKSHA APP Questions

☐ Multiple Choice Questions

Q.1 Name the parasitic nematode which infects the roots of tobacco plants?

(a) *Trichoderma*   (b) *Agrobacterium tumifaciens*
(c) *Bacillus thurigiensis*   (d) *Meloidegyne incognitia*

Sol. (d) *Meloidogyne incognita*, also known as the root knot nematode, infects the roots of tobacco plants, causing damage and reducing crop yield.

Q.2 Name a bacterial gene which is used to produce insect resistant plant?

(a) *Bt.* toxin gene   (b) Gene for α-I-antitrypsin
(c) Gene encoding hirudin   (d) Gene for ADA

Sol. (a) The Bt toxin gene (from *Bacillus thuringiensis*) is used to produce insect-resistant plants by encoding a protein that is toxic to specific insect pests.

Q.3 Which insect is controlled by gene *Cry*IIAb?

(a) Corn borer   (b) Cotton bollworms
(c) Fruit borer   (d) Maize stem borer

Sol. (b) The *cry*IIAb gene from *Bacillus thuringiensis* is used to control the cotton bollworms, a pest that damages corn crops by producing a protein toxic to the insect.

Q.4 Silencing the translation of the *m*RNA is done by the process of

(a) gene therapy (b) amplification (c) RNA interference (d) elution

Sol. (c) RNA interference (RNAi) is the process that silences the translation of *m*RNA, preventing the expression of specific genes by degrading or inhibiting *m*RNA.

Q.5 A collection of methods that allows correction of a gene defect in a child/embryo is called as

(a) Gene therapy   (b) Silencing
(c) ELISA test   (d) Electrophoresis

Sol. (a) Gene therapy is a technique that involves altering or replacing defective genes within a person's cells to treat or prevent genetic disorders.

Q.6 What is the permanent cure for ADA deficiency?

(a) Enzyme replacement Therapy

(b) Bone marrow transplantation

(c) Introduction of the gene isolated from marrow cell producing ADA at early embryonic stage

(d) Introduction of lymphocytes containing functional ADA *c*DNA into the patient.

Sol. (c) The permanent cure for ADA (adenosine deaminase) deficiency is gene therapy, where a functional copy of the ADA gene is introduced into the patient's cells to restore immune function.

Q.7 Which method will help in the early diagnosis of a disease?

(a) Screen analysis

(b) Selectable marker

(c) Urine analysis

(d) Polymerase chain reaction

Sol. (d) PCR helps in the early diagnosis of a disease by amplifying specific DNA sequences, allowing detection of pathogens or genetic mutations at an early stage.

Q.8 Which enzyme produced by Thermus aquaticus is used for amplification of genes using PCR?

(a) RNA polymerase   (b) DNA ligase

(c) *Taq* polymerase   (d) Endonuclease

Sol. (c) *Taq* polymerase, produced by *Thermus aquaticus,* is used for gene amplification in PCR due to its ability to withstand the high temperatures required for DNA denaturation.

Q.9 Transgenic animals are used to produce medicines required to treat certain human diseases. Which of the following is produced by transgenic animal?

(a) *cry* gene   (b) α-I-antitrypsin

(c) *Bt* toxin   (d) Vitamin-A

Sol. (b) α-I-antitrypsin is produced by transgenic animals, such as goats or cows, and is used to treat diseases like emphysema caused by a deficiency in this protein.

☐ Very Short Answer Type

Q.1 GM plants have been useful in many ways. Explain how?

Sol. Plants whose genes have been altered by manipulation are called Genetically Modified plants (GM plants). GM plants have been useful in many ways. Genetic modification has following advantages.

1. These plants are resistant to abiotic stresses. These plants can survive in tough climates, like extreme heat or cold, drought, or high salinity.

2. GM technology can be used to boost the vitamins and minerals in crops, making them healthier to eat. For example- golden rice is rich in vitamin A. These plants can more efficiently utilise soil minerals and prevent early exhaustion of fertility of soil.

3. These plants are resistant to various diseases, which are caused by bacteria, fungi, viruses etc.

4. GM plants are pest resistant. GM plants are better at fighting off bugs and diseases, so they can reduce the utilisation of chemical insecticides or pesticides e.g., Bt cotton.

5. GM plants have helped to reduce post harvest losses.

Q.2 Why is production of mature form of insulin using *r*DNA technique a challenge? How is the challenge overcome by Eli Lilly company?

Sol. In humans, immature pro-insulin contains A, Band C-peptide chains. The C peptide is not present in the mature insulin and is removed during maturation into insulin. The main challenge for production of insulin using *r*DNA technique was getting insulin assembled into a mature form. In 1983, Eli Lilly, an American company, first prepared two DNA sequences corresponding to A and B chains of human insulin and introduced them in plasmids of *E. coli* to produce insulin chains. Chains A and B were produced separately, extracted and combined by creating disulphide bonds to form human insulin (humulin).

Organisms and Populations

CHAPTER 11

Important Points

01 Ecology is the study of the relationships of living organisms with the abiotic and biotic components of their environment. It is concerned with four levels of biological organisation.

  (i) Organisms
  (ii) Populations
  (iii) Communities
  (iv) Biomes.

02 Populations A population is constituted of organisms, which are living in groups in a well defined geographical area share or compete for similar resources and interbreed through sexual reproduction or reproduce asexually.

Population contain certain attributes that are not seen in an individual organism. These include population density, birth rate, death rate and sex ratio.

03 Age Pyramid refers to a graphical representation of the age distribution (per cent individuals of a given age or age group) plotted for the population.

The shape of the pyramids reflects the growth status of the population and is of three types *i.e.*, (a) Growing (b) Stable (c) Declining.

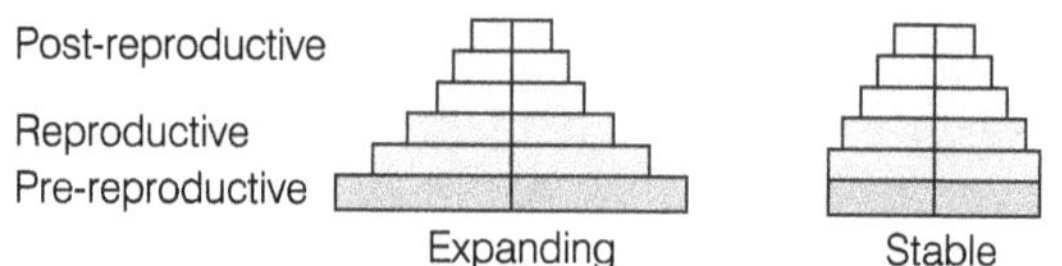

▲ Representation of age pyramids for human population

04 Population Growth The size of a population for any species keeps changing with time, depending on various factors including food availability, predation pressure and weather conditions.

05 The density of a population in a given habitat during a given period, fluctuates due to changes in four basic processes, two of which (natality and immigration contribute to an increase in population density and two (mortality and emigration) to a decrease.

Population Density is given by following equation.

$$N_{t+1} = N_t + [(B + I) - (D + E)]$$

where, N_{t+1} = population density at a time $t + 1$, B = birth rate
I = immigration, D = death rate, E = emigration,
N_t = population in the beginning

06 Growth Models Growth models tell us about the patterns of growth of a population with time.

- There are two models of population growth *i.e.,* exponential growth and logistic growth.
- The exponential growth is common when the resources are unlimited whereas when the resources become limited, the population grow logistically.
- When population density is plotted in relation to time, a J- shape (exponential) or sigmoid curve (logistic) as obtained.

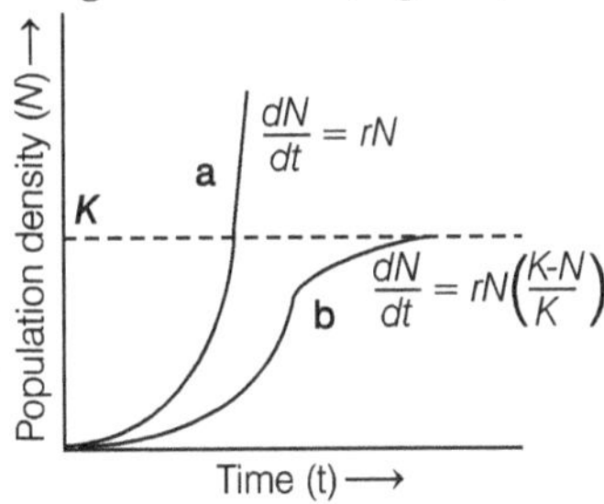

Populatin growth curve

    a When responses are not limiting the growth, plot is exoponential,

    b When responses are limiting the growth, plot is logistic,

    K Ps carrying capacity

$$\frac{dN}{dt} = \text{Rate of change in population size}$$

$$\frac{K - N}{k} = \text{Environmental resistanece}$$

$$r = \text{Intrinsic rate of natural increase}$$

07 Population Interactions

(i) Interspecific interactions arise from the interaction of populations of two different species. They could be beneficial, detrimental or neutral (neither harm nor benefit) to one of the species or both.

(ii) The possible outcomes of interspecific interactions are depict in the table given below.

Species A	Species B	Name of Interaction
+	+	Mutualism
–	–	Competition
+	–	Predation
+	–	Parasitism
+	0	Commensalism
–	0	Amensalism

(a) Predation

- In this interaction, an organism called **predator**, kills and consumes, the other weaker organism called **prey**.
- Predators keep prey populations under control and do not let them achieve very high population densities and cause ecosystem instability.
- Prey species have evolved various defenses to lessen the impact of predation, for *e.g.*, Some species of insects and frogs are cryptically coloured (camouflaged), mimic natural object to fool the predator.

(b) Competition

- It occurs due to limited resources between closely related species.
- It is a type of interaction, where both the species suffer. It may exist between same species intraspecific competition or between individuals of different species (interspecific competition). *e.g.*, in some shallow South African lakes, visiting flamingos and resident fishes compete for their common food and zooplankton.
- **Competitive release** states the phenomenon of a species whose distribution is restricted to a small geographical area because of the presence of a competitively superior species. It is found to expand its distribution range dramatically when the competing species are experimentally removed.

- **Gause's competitive exclusion principle** states that two closely related species competing for the same resources cannot co-exist indefinitely and the competitively inferior one will be eliminated eventually by the superior one.
- **Resource partioning** refers to the phenomenon in which species facing competition might evolve, mechanisms that promote co-existence rather than exclusion.

(c) **Parasitism** It is the mode of interaction between two species in which one species (parasite) depends on the other species (host) for food and shelter. In this process, parasite damages the host and benefits itself.

- Life cycles of some parasites are complex, where one or more intermediate host or vectors that facilitate parasitisation are present, *e.g.* Malarial parasite (*Plasmodium*) needs a vector (mosquito) to complete its life cycle.
- **Types of parasites** parasites can be of two types, *i.e.* that feed on the external surface of the host organism, (Ectoparasite) *e.g.* lice on humans and ticks on dogs and *Cuscuta*, etc. that live inside the host body at different sites (Endoparasite) *e.g.*, tapeworm.
- **Brood parasitism** is a phenomenon in which one organism (parasite) lays its eggs in the next of another organism or host and let the host incubate them, *e.g.* Cuckoo bird lays its eggs in the nest of its host and lets the host incubate them.

(d) **Commensalism** This is the interaction in which one species is benefited without affecting the other, *e.g.*, an orchid growing as an epiphyte on a mango branch.

(e) **Mutualism** This interaction confers benefits on both the interacting species, *e.g.*, *Lichen*, *mycorrhizae*.

(f) **Amensalism** It defines the interaction between two different species in which one species is harmed and other is neither benefitted nor harmed.

Exercises

Question 1 List the attributes that populations but not individuals possess.

Sol. A population has the following attributes that an individual does not possess

   (i) birth rates and death rates   (ii) sex ratio

  (iii) population density   (iv) age distribution

   (v) population growth   (vi) population dispersal.

Question 2 If a population growing exponentially double in size in 3 years, what is the intrinsic rate of increase (r) of the population?

Sol. The intrinsic rate of increase (r) of the population is measured by the formula

$$N_t = N_o e^{rt} \qquad \text{... (i)}$$

Where, $N_t = 2x$, $N_0 = x$, $t = 3$

$\therefore$ From equation (i)

In

$$\frac{N_t = \ln N_0 + 1ne^{rt}}{\ln No + \int rt\ 1ne}$$

$$\ln No + rt\ (1ne = 1)$$

or

$$r = \frac{\ln N_t - 1n\ No}{t} \quad \text{or} \quad r = \frac{\ln N_t / No}{t},$$

or

$$rt = 2.303 \log \frac{2x}{x} \qquad \left[\therefore 1n\ \frac{2x}{x} = 2.303 \log_{10} \frac{2x}{x} \right]$$

or

$$r = \frac{2.303 \times 0.301}{3} = \frac{0.6931}{3} = 0.231 \text{ or } 23.1\%$$

Question 3 Name important defense mechanisms in plants against herbivory.

Sol. The important defense mechanisms in plants against the herbivory are as follows

  (i) Thorns, prickles, spines, etc., on stems and leaves that can injure or kill the grazer.

 (ii) Many plants produce and store chemicals that make the herbivore sick when they are eaten. They disrupt their feeding habit or digestion or even kill it.

(iii) Defensive compounds like resins, wax, lignins, nicotine, quinine released by plant body, act as repellants against grazers and browsers.

(iv) Some plant produces highly poisonous cardiac glycosides, *e.g.*, *Calotropis*.

 (v) Some plants have sticky glandular hair, shining hair or heavily coating.

Question 4 An orchid plant is growing on the branch of mango tree. How do you describe this interaction between the orchid and the mango tree?

Sol. An orchid growing as an epiphyte on a branch of mango tree is an example of commensalism. The orchids use trees only for attachment and manufacture their own food by photosynthesis whereas the mango tree is neither harmed hor benefited.

Question 5 What is the ecological principle behind the biological control method of managing with pest insects?

Sol. The ecological principle behind the biological control method of managing with pest insects is through their natural enemies. Biological control of pests is largely based on predator-prey relation. **Example**-Fish *Gamubsia* is introduced in ponds to check growth of mosquito larvae. Baculoviruses are useful in controlling many insects and other arthropods. Aphids and other pests are kept under check by beetles.

Question 6 Define population and community.

Sol. **Population** It is a group of individuals of same species which can reproduce among themselves and occupy a particular area in a given time.

Community It is an assemblage of populations of different species the same geographical parea which interacts through competition, predation mutualism, etc.

Question 7 Define the following terms and give one example for each
(a) Commensalism (b) Parasitism (c) Camouflage (d) Mutualism
(e) Interspecific competition

Sol. (a) **Commensalism** It is an interaction between two different species, where one is benefitted and other remains unaffected.

e.g., Clown fish and sea anemone. The clown fish gets protection from predators which stay away from stinging tentacles of anemone but anemone does not derive any benefit from fish.

(b) **Parasitism** It is an interaction between two organsims in which one is benefitted by obtaining nourishment and spends apart or whole life on or inside the body of other organisms and other is harmed.

e.g., Cuscuta, a parasite plant that is found growing on hedge plants, do not have chlorophyll and thus, derives its nutrition from the host.

(c) **Camouflage** It is a phenomenon of blending of an organism with the surrounding due to similar colour, marking and shape so, as to avoid the predators. *e.g.,* Leaf-like insect such as grasshopper.

(d) **Mutualism** The interaction between two species in which, both organisms are benefited to maintain the life process is called mutualism.

e.g., In lichens, fungi helps in absorption of nutrients and water while the algal partner manufactures food.

(e) **Interspecific competition** It is the competition among the members of different species for limited natural resources. *e.g.,* The Abingdon tortoise in Galapagos islands became extinct within a decade after goats were introduced on the Island, apparently due to the greater browsing efficiency of the goats.

Question 8 With the help of suitable diagram describe the logistic population growth curve.

Sol. Logistic population growth curve

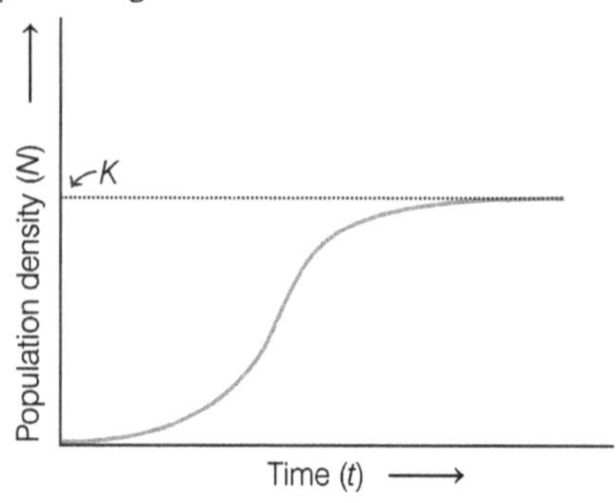

Population growth curve

(i) When the resources become limited at certain point of time, no population can grow exponentially.

(ii) This growth model is realistic.

(iii) Every ecosystem or environment has limited resources to support a particular maximum number of individual called its carrying capacity (K).

(iv) When N is plotted in relation to time t, the logistic growth curve shows, the sigmoid curve and is also called. **Verhulst-Pearl logistic growth.** It is given by the following equation :

$$\frac{dN}{dt} = rN \left[\frac{K - N}{K} \right]$$

where, N = population density at time t

r = intrinsic rate of natural increase

K = carrying capacity

Question 9 Select the statement which explains best parasitism.

(a) One organism is benefited.

(b) Both the organisms are benefited.

(c) One organism is benefited, other is not affected.

(d) One organism is benefited, other is affected.

Sol. (d) The statement in option (d), best explains parasitism as it is a type of symbiotic relationship between two species where one organism is benefitted and other is affected.

Question 10 List any three important characteristics of a population and explain.

Sol. The three important characteristics of a population are
   (i) **Population density** The number of individuals of a species per unit area or a volume is called population density.
   (ii) **Birth rate** It is expressed as the number of births per 1000 individuals of a population per year.
   (iii) **Death rate** It is expressed as the number of deaths per 1000 individuals of a population per year.

DIKSHA APP Questions

☐ Short Answer Type

Q.1 Justify the statement

"Besides acting as conduits for energy transfer across trophic levels Predator play other important roles in an ecosystem".

Sol. Apart from acting as a conduits for energy transfer across trophic level, predators play the following roles in an ecosystem
- They keep the prey population under control and maintain ecosystem stability.
- They also help in maintaining species diversity in a community by reducing the intensity of competition among competing prey species.

Q.2 Given an example for a symbiotic relationship existing between a plant and a pollinating agent. How it is mutually benefited?

Sol. An example of a symbiotic relationship can be seen the fig tree and the wasp. The wasp lays its eggs inside the figs flower and in return it pollinates the fig. The plant also provides some of its developing seeds as a food for the developing was larvae.

Hence, both the species are mutually benefitted.

Q.3 Name the floral rewards a biotic agent is getting from a flower?

Sol. The floral reward a biotic agent may get from a flower are nectar, pollen grains and space to lay eggs.

Ecosystem

CHAPTER 12

Important Points

01 Ecosystem is a functional unit of nature, an association of organisms and their physical environment, interconnected by a continuous flow of energy and a cycling of nutrients.

02 An ecosystem varies greatly in size from a small pond to a large forest or a sea.

03 Ecosystem can be divided into two categories, namely the terrestrial and the aquatic.

04 Crop fields and an aquarium are the examples of man-made ecosystems.

05 Every ecosystem has inputs and outputs of energy and nutrients.

06 Energy cannot be recycled; therefore, a constant input of energy from the sun, is required to sustain all the ecosystems.

07 Structure of Ecosystem Ecosystems consist of interacting biotic and abiotic components, with energy flow linking them. Each ecosystem has a unique physical structure and species composition. Vertical distribution of species, called stratification, includes trees in the top layer, shrubs in the middle, and herbs or grasses at the bottom.

08 Components of Ecosystem Ecosystem components function as a unit through productivity, decomposition, energy flow, and nutrient cycling.

Example of an ecosystem—A pond

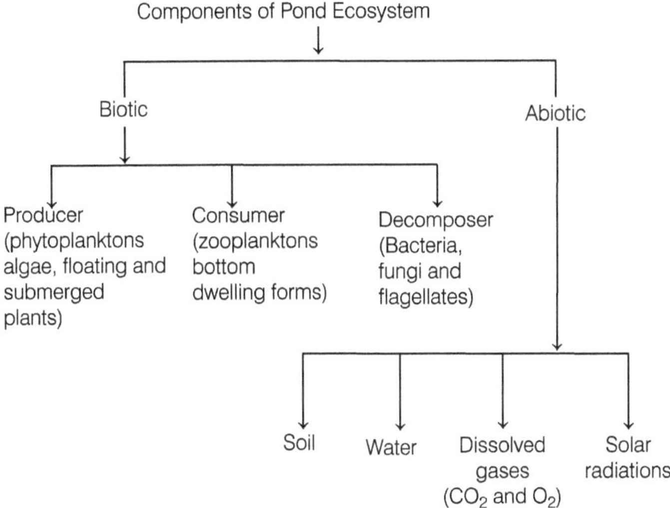

09 Functioning of Ecosystem Ecosystems convert inorganic substance to organic matter via autotrophs, support heterotrophs through consumption of autotrophs, recycle nutrients via decomposition, and ensure unidirectional energy flow with heat loss to the environment.

10 Primary Production Primary production is the biomass produced by plants per unit area over time during photosynthesis, expressed as weight or energy.

(i) Productivity refers to the rate of biomass production, measured annually.

(ii) Productivity can be divided into **Gross Primary Productivity (GPP)** and **Net Primary Productivity** (NPP).

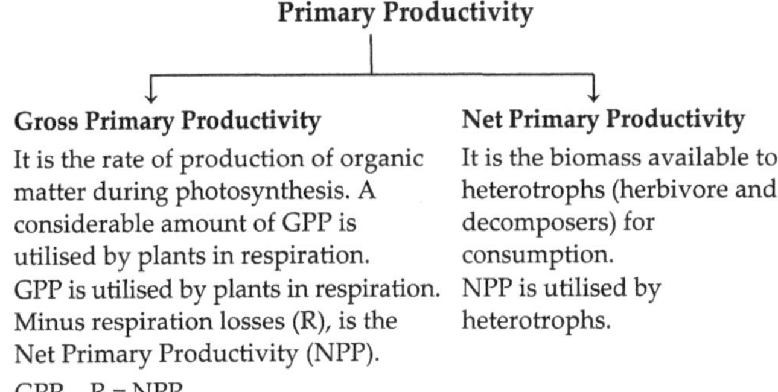

Primary Productivity

Gross Primary Productivity	**Net Primary Productivity**
It is the rate of production of organic matter during photosynthesis. A considerable amount of GPP is utilised by plants in respiration. GPP is utilised by plants in respiration. Minus respiration losses (R), is the Net Primary Productivity (NPP). $GPP - R = NPP$	It is the biomass available to heterotrophs (herbivore and decomposers) for consumption. NPP is utilised by heterotrophs.

(iii) **Primary productivity** depends on plant species, environmental factors, nutrients, and photosynthetic capacity, varying across ecosystems. The biosphere's annual NPP is ~170 billion tons, with oceans contributing only 55 billion tons despite covering 70% of Earth's surface.

(iv) **Secondary productivity** is defined as the rate of formation of new organic matter by consumers.

11 **Decomposition** Decomposition is the breakdown of complex organic matter into simpler inorganic substances by decomposers. Detritus (dead plant/animal remains) is the raw material for decomposition which undergoes **fragmentation, leaching, catabolism, humification,** and **mineralisation.**

Fragmentation breaks detritus into smaller particles, leaching removes soluble nutrients, and catabolism degrades matter into simpler substances. **Humification** forms humus, a nutrient-rich substance, which is slowly decomposed by microbes. **Mineralisation** releases inorganic nutrients from humus, completing the nutrient cycle.

12 **Factors Affecting Decomposition** It include the chemical composition of detritus (rich in lignin and chitin slows it, while nitrogen and sugars speed it up), and climatic factors like temperature and moisture. Warm, moist conditions promote decomposition, while low temperature and anaerobic conditions slow it down, leading to organic material buildup.

13 **Energy flow** refers to the transfer of energy through an ecosystem, from producers to consumers. Energy flows unidirectionally from the sun to producers, then to consumers. Plants use photosynthetically active radiation (PAR) to synthesise food, while animals, as consumers, obtain energy from plants. This energy transfer is represented by food chains.

14 A food chain is a sequence of organisms where each serves as a source of food for the next, transferring energy and nutrients. There are two types of food chains:

- **Grazing Food Chain (GFC)** Starts with living plants, progresses through herbivores to carnivores.
- **Detritus Food Chain (DFC)** Begins with dead organic matter, involving decomposers that break it down into simpler substances.
- The natural connections among food chains create a complex food web.

15 **Trophic Level**, each organism occupies a particular position in the food chain, called a trophic level. Example- Producers occupy the first trophic level, herbivores (primary consumers) the second, and carnivores (secondary consumers) the third.

- Each trophic level has a specific amount of living material at any given time, known as the **standing crop.** This is typically measured as the **biomass** of living organisms or the number of organisms per unit area.
- In a grazing food chain, the number of trophic levels is limited by the 10 percent law, where only 10 percent of energy is transferred to each higher level.

16 **Ecological Pyramid** An ecological pyramid graphically represents ecological parameters like number, biomass, and energy across trophic levels in a food chain. Producers are at the base, followed by herbivores and carnivores at higher levels. Ecological pyramids can be upright, inverted, or spindleshaped.

There are of three types:
- **Pyramid of Number** Shows the number of individuals at each trophic level. It is typically upright but can be inverted, as in case of large trees.
- **Pyramid of Biomass** Represents the biomass at each level, usually upright, but inverted in aquatic food chains involving short-lived organisms like plankton.
- **Pyramid of Energy** Represents the energy captured at each trophic level. It is always upright due to energy loss at each transfer stage.

Exercises

Question 1 Fill in the blanks.

   (a) Plants are called as .... because they fix carbon dioxide.

   (b) In an ecosystem dominated by trees, the pyramid (of numbers) is......... type.

   (c) In aquatic ecosystems, the limiting factor for the productivity is ....

   (d) Common detritivores in our ecosystem are......... .

   (e) The major reservoir of carbon on earth is......... .

Sol. (a) Plants are called as **producers** because they fix carbon dioxide.

   (b) In an ecosystem dominated by trees, the pyramid (of numbers) is **upright** type.

   (c) In aquatic ecosystems, the limiting factor for the productivity is **sunlight.**

   (d) Common detritivores in our ecosystem are **earthworm.**

   (e) The major reservoir of carbon on earth is **oceans.**

Question 2 Which one of the following has the largest population in a food chain?

   (a) Producers   (b) Primary consumers

   (c) Secondary consumers   (d) Decomposers

Sol. (a) Producers have the largest population in a food chain.

Question 3 The second trophic level in a lake is

   (a) phytoplankton   (b) zooplankton

   (c) benthos   (d) fishes

Sol. (b) Zooplankton is the second trophic level in a lake.

Question 4 Secondary producers are

   (a) herbivores   (b) producers

   (c) carnivores   (d) None of these

Sol. (d) None of these

Question 5 What is the percentage of Photosynthetically Active Radiation (PAR) in the incident solar radiation?

   (a) 100%   (b) 50 %   (c) 1-5%   (d) 2-10%

Sol. (b) 50 % of the incident solar radiation is Photosynthetically Active Radiation (PAR).

Question 6 Distinguish between
(a) grazing food chain and detritus food chain
(b) production and decomposition
(c) upright and inverted pyramid
(d) food chain and food web
(e) litter and detritus
(f) primary and secondary productivity

Sol.

(a)

S.N.	Grazing Food Chain	Detritus Food Chain
1.	Food chain in which energy flows from plants to herbivores and then through carnivores.	Where energy flows from photosynthetic organisms through detritivores and decomposers.
2.	Begins with producers at the first trophic level.	Begins with detritivores and decomposers as the first trophic level.
3.	Sun's energy is fixed by producers and is made available to consumers.	Energy from the organic matter is used up by decomposers and detritivores and nutrients are made available for reuse by producers.
4.	It supports detrital food chain.	It supports grazing food chain by providing inorganic nutrients.

(b)

S.N.	Production	Decomposition
1.	Process of synthesis of organic matter or biomass from inorganic matter using radiant energy by plants.	Process of breakdown of complex organic matter into inorganic substances by decomposers so that they can be reused.
2.	It fixes energy.	It releases energy and nutrients.

(c)

S.N.	Upright Pyramid	Inverted Pyramid
1.	Pyramid is upright when the number of producers or their biomass is maximum and decreases at each trophic level in a food chain.	Pyramid is inverted when the number of organism or their biomass at producer level is minimum and increases at each trophic level in a food chain.
2.	Pyramid of energy is always upright.	Pyramid of numbers in tree ecosystem and pyramid of biomass is inverted in aquatic system.

(d)

S.N.	Food Chain	Food Web
1.	A linear sequence showing food energy flow in the ecosystem.	Comprises of a number of cross connecting food chains through which food energy flows in the ecosystem.
2.	Organisms of higher trophic level feed on a single type of organism of lower trophic level.	Organisms of higher trophic level feed on a number of alternative organisms of lower trophic level.

(e)

S.N.	Litter	Detritus
1.	It is made up of dried fallen plant matter and animal faecal matter.	It is made up of dead plants and animals.

(f)

S.N.	Primary Productivity	Secondary Productivity
1.	The rate at which primary producers capture and store a given amount of energy in their tissues, in a given time interval.	It is the rate of formation of new organic matter by consumers.
2.	It is comparatively much larger.	It is much less and decreases with rise of trophic level.
3.	Fresh organic matter synthesised from inorganic raw material.	Synthesis of new organic matter from pre-synthesised organic matter.

Question 7 Describe the components of an ecosystem.

Sol. An ecosystem consists of two components— abiotic and biotic.

Abiotic component include the physical environmental factors, *e.g.,* the water, soil, wind, sunlight, etc.

Biotic component includes

(i) **Primary producers** or **the autotrophs**, *e.g.,* plants, phytoplankton, some algae, etc., that can use sunlight to make food.

(ii) **Primary consumers** feed on the producers, the plants. The primary consumers are all **herbivores**.

Some common herbivores are insects, birds and mammals in terrestrial ecosystem and molluscs in aquatic ecosystem.

(iii) **Secondary consumers** are animals, which eat plant eating animals.

The consumers that feed on these herbivores are **primary carnivores** (though secondary consumers), *e.g.* spiders, beetles and birds.

(iv) **Tertiary consumers** eat secondary consumers. Animals that depend on the primary carnivores for food are labelled as **secondary carnivores**, *e.g.,* owl, eagle and fox.

(v) **The decomposers** are heterotrophic organisms, mainly fungi, bacteria and other small organisms that breakdown the complex organic matter into inorganic substances like carbon dioxide, water and nutrients.

(vi) **Detritivores** *e.g.,* earthworm, slugs, crabs and insects that breakdown detritus such as leaves, bark, flowers and dead remains of animals, including faecal matter into smaller particles.

Question 8 Define ecological pyramids and describe with examples, pyramids of number and biomass.

Sol. Ecological pyramids are graphical representations of the relationship between organisms of different trophic levels that can be expressed in terms of number, biomass or energy.

In most ecosystems, the pyramid of number is upright, *i.e.,* producers are more in number than the herbivores and herbivores are more in number than the carnivores. But, the pyramid may be inverted as in a forest ecosystem, where the number of insects (primary consumers) are greater than the number of trees (producers).

The pyramid of biomass is also upright, generally, as the biomass of producers is more than biomass of herbivores and that of herbivores is more than biomass of carnivores. But, it is inverted in many ecosystems like in sea ecosystem, where the biomass of fishes (primary consumers) far exceeds biomass of phytoplankton (producers).

Question 9 What is primary productivity? Give brief description of factors that affect primary productivity.

Sol. Primary productivity is defined as the amount of biomass or organic matter produced per unit over a time period by plants during photosynthesis. It is expressed in terms of weight (gm^{-2}) or energy $(Kcalm^{-2})$.

Primary productivity depends on

(i) the plant species inhabiting a particular area.

(ii) the environmental factors like sunlight, temperature and moisture.

(iii) availability of nutrients.

(iv) photosynthetic capacity of plants.

Question 10 Define decomposition and describe the processes and products of decomposition.

Sol. **Decomposition** is the process of breakdown of complex organic matter into inorganic substances so that they can be reused. It is carried out by organisms called decomposers.

Products of decomposition are carbon dioxide, water and nutrients.

The important steps in the process of decomposition are

 (i) **Fragmentation** Breakdown of detritus (dead plant remains and dead remains of animals) into smaller particles by detritivores (*e.g.,* earthworm).

 (ii) **Leaching** Water soluble inorganic nutrients go down into the soil horizon and get precipitated as unavailable salts.

(iii) **Catabolism** Bacterial and fungal enzymes degrade detritus into simpler inorganic substances.

(iv) **Humification** Accumulation of a dark-coloured amorphous substance, which acts as a reservior of nutrients for plants.

 (v) **Mineralisation** Humus is further degraded by some microbes and release of inorganic nutrients into the soil.

Question 11 Give an account of energy flow in an ecosystem.

Sol. In an ecosystem a constant supply of energy is required. The passage of energy through various trophic levels of an ecosystem is called energy flow. There is no circulation ofenergy instead unidirectional flow of energy occurs in the ecosystem.

 (i) Sun is the only source of energy for all ecosystems on earth.

 (ii) Plants, photosynthetic and chemosynthetic bacteria (producers), fix energy from solar radiation and store it in their tissues.

(iii) All organisms are dependent for their food on plants, either directly or indirectly. It means there is a unidirectional flow of energy from the sun to producers and then to consumers.

(iv) The energy trapped by the producer, is either passed on to a consumer or to the decomposer (in case the plant dies) through two types of food chains—grazing food chain and detritus food chain that cross connect many times.

Only 10% of energy is transferred from one trophic level to the next. The remaining 90% of this energy is used by plants for various processes like growth, reproduction, etc. This is known as 10% law of energy flow.

☐ **Multiple Choice Questions**

Q.1 Of the following which ecosystem will show lowest primary productivity?

(a) Marsh   (b) Desert

(c) Swamp   (d) Tropical rainforest

Sol. (b) Deserts generally show the lowest primary productivity due to limited water availability and harsh environmental conditions, which restrict plant growth.

Q.2 Breakdown of detritus into smaller particles is called

(a) leaching   (b) mineralisation

(c) fragmentation   (d) decomposition

Sol. (c) Fragmentation is the process where detritus is broken down into smaller particles, usually by detritivores like insects or earthworms, which aids in further decomposition.

Q.3 If plants and other producers are removed from ecosystem result would be

(a) ecosystem collapse

(b) number of consumers will increase

(c) carbon dioxide level will decrease

(d) number of consumers will not be affected

Sol. (a) If plants and other producers are removed from an ecosystem, it would lead to ecosystem collapse, as producers are the foundation of the food chain, and their absence would disrupt the entire system's energy flow and biodiversity.

Q.4 Which one of the following is not used for construction of ecological pyramid?

(a) Biomass   (b) Fresh weight

(c) Energy flow   (d) Number of individuals

Sol. (b) Fresh weight is not typically used for the construction of ecological pyramids. Instead, biomass, energy flow, and number of individuals are used to represent the structure and functioning of ecosystems in terms of ecological pyramids.

Q.5 Which among the following ecological pyramids is always upright?

(a) Pyramid of energy   (b) Pyramid of biomass
(c) Pyramid of number   (d) Pyramid of magnitude

Sol. (a) The pyramid of energy is always upright because energy decreases as it flows from producers to consumers, following the law of energy conservation.

☐ Short Answer Type

Q.1 What are the ecosystem services of a healthy forest ecosystem?

Sol. A healthy forest ecosystem provides essential services, including purifying air and water, regulating water cycles to mitigate droughts and floods, and recycling nutrients to create fertile soil. It offers habitats for diverse species, supporting biodiversity, and aids in crop pollination. Forests act as carbon sinks, absorbing CO_2 and helps to fight climate change. Additionally, they hold aesthetic, cultural, and spiritual value, enriching human life. These interconnected services play a critical role in maintaining ecological balance and supporting both environmental and human well-being.

Q.2 What is the reason for the low productivity of oceans compared to land?

Sol. The reason for low productivity of oceans as compared to land is that in oceans, the limiting factor for productivity is light. The producers are dependent on light, which does not reach the deeper layers of the ocean but in available in large quantities on land. Also, the amount of minerals and nutrients present in the ocean water is low as compared to land.

Q.3 Is there any limitation to the number of trophic levels in a detritus food chain?

Sol. In a detritus food chain, there is no strict limit on the number of trophic levels because energy flows continuously through decomposers, rather than in distinct steps between separate organisms, as in a grazing food chain.

Biodiversity and Conservation

CHAPTER 13

Important Points

01 Biodiversity is the term used to describe the sum total of the diversity at all levels of biological organisation ranging from organic molecules within the cell to biomass.

The three most important levels of biodiversity are Genetic diversity, Species diversity, Ecological diversity.

02 Patterns of Biodiversity The diversity of plants and animals, throughout the world, is not evenly distributed and shows some interesting patterns of distribution.

  (i) **Latitudinal gradients** means that, species diversity decreases as we move away from the equator towards the poles.

  (a) Greater biodiversity is observed in tropics because

  - the temperate regions were subjected to frequent glaciations in the past, whereas tropical latitudes remained undisturbed and thus, had a long evolutionary time for species diversification.
  - Unlike temparate regions, tropical environment are less seasonal more constant and predictable. Such constant environment promote niche specialisation and lead to a greater species diversity.
  - Tropics have greater solar energy exposure which contributes to highter productivity and greater diversity.
  - High humidity and high temperature provide favourable conditions for mass species.

(ii) **Species-area relationships** Alexander von Humboldt observed that within a region species richness increased with the increasing explored area, but only up to a limit.

   (a) The relation between species richness and area, for a wide variety of taxa is a rectangular hyperbola.

   On a logarithmic scale, the relationship is a straight line described by the equation

   $$\log S = \log C + Z \log A$$

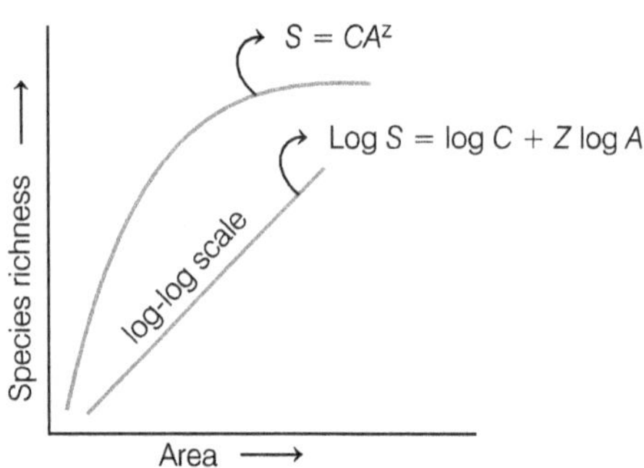

▲ Showing species area relationship

   where, S = species richness, A = area, Z = slope of the line (regression coefficient) and C = Y-intercept.

   (b) The value of z lies in the range of 0.1 to 0.2 regardless of the taxonomic group or the region.

   (c) However the analysis of very large areas like the entire continents, gives steep slope of line. (Z values that ranges from 0.6 to 1.2)

03 The Importance of Species Diversity to the Ecosystem

   (i) For several years ecologist believed that communities with more species diversity, generally, tend to be more stable than those with less species. This was confirmed by David Tilman.

   (ii) A stable community shown less variation in productivity is resistant to occasional disturbances and resists invasion by alien species.

   (iii) Importance of biodiversity for survival of species can be explained by the rivet popper hypothesis'.proposed by Paul Ehlrich.

   (iv) This hypothesis assumes the ecosystem to be an airplane and the species to be the rivets joining all parts together.

04 Loss of Biodiversity

(i) The IUCN Red List (2004) documents the extinction of 784 species (including 338 vertebrates, 359 invertebrates and 87 plants) in the last 500 years.

(ii) Some examples of recent extinctions include the dodo (Mauritius), quagga (Africa), thylacine (Australia), Steller's Sea Cow (Russia) and three sub-species (Bali, Javan, Caspian) of tiger.

(iii) The loss of biodiversity in a region may lead to decline in plant production, lowered resistance of plants to environmental disturbances and negative impact on ecosystem processes such as plant productivity, water use, pest and disease cycles.

05 Causes of Biodiversity Loss

There are four major causes of biodiversity loss. These are known as 'The evil Quartet.

(i) **Habitat loss and fragmentation** Population explosion, pollution, urbanisation and industrialisation have destroyed forest land, which is the primary cause of extinction of species.

(ii) **Over-exploitation** When the biological system is over exploited by man for the natural resources, it results in degradation and extinction of species.

(iii) **Alien species invasions** When alien species are introduced unintentionally or deliberately in a habitat, some of them can cause decline or extinction of indigenous species.

(iv) **Co-extinctions** When a species becomes extinct, the plant and animal species associated with it, in an obligatory way, also become extinct.

06 Biodiversity Conservation

There are a number of reasons to conserve biodiversity that can be grouped into three categories—**narrowly utilitarian, broadly utilitarian** and **ethical.**

(i) **The narrowly utilitarian** arguments for conserving biodiversity are that humans derive numerous direct economic benefits from nature such as food product firewood, fibre, construction material industrial products (tannins, dyes, resins, etc.,) and medicinally important products.

(ii) **The broadly utilitarian** view is that biodiversity plays a major role in many ecosystem services which in turn provides us with benefits such as aesthetic value, oxygen climate regulation etc.

(iii) **The ethical argument** for conserving biodiversity relates to our moral obligation to conserve the planet that we share with millions of plant, animal and microbe species.

07 Conservation of Biodiversity There are two basic approaches in the conservation of biodiversity. These are *in situ* conservation and *ex situ* conservation.

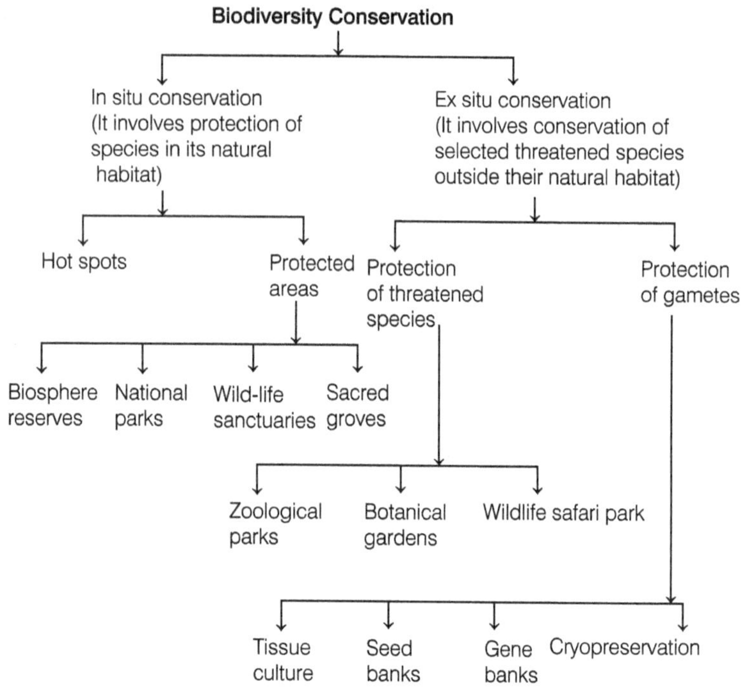

08 Conventions on Biodiversity

(i) The Earth Summit was held in Rio de Janeiro in 1992 which called upon all nations to take appropriate measures for conservation of biodiversity and sustainable utilisation of its benefits.

(ii) The World Summit on Sustainable development held in 2002 in Johannesburg, South Africa in which 190 countries pledged to reduce the current rate of biodiversity loss at global, regional and local levels by 2010.

Exercises

Question 1 Name the three important components of biodiversity.

Sol. Three important components of biodiversity are genetic diversity, species diversity and ecological diversity.

Question 2 How do ecologists estimate the total number of species present in the world?

Sol. Ecologists make a statistical comparison of the species richness of systematically studied groups of insects of the temperate and tropical regions and extrapolate this ratio to other groups of animals and plants. This gives the gross estimate of the total number of species existing on this planet and other method is by rate of discovery of new species.

Question 3 Give three hypothesis for explaining why tropics show greatest levels of species richness?

Sol. The three hypothesis for explaining why tropics show greatest levels of species richness are as follows.

(i) Speciation is generally a function of time and environmental stability. The temperate regions were subjected to frequent glaciations in the past, whereas tropical latitudes have remained relatively undisturbed for millions of years and thus, had a long evolutionary time for species diversification.

(ii) Tropical environment provide continued favourable seasons that are relatively more constant and predictable. Such constant environment promote niche specialisation and lead to a greater species diversity.

(iii) The availability of more solar energy in the tropics, contributes to higher productivity; which in turn might contribute indirectly to greater diversity.

Question 4 What is the significance of the slope of regression in a species-area relationship?

Sol. Slope of regression or regression coefficient makes it easier to measure species richness along an area. When the analysis of species-area relationship is done, in a small areas, the values of slopes of regression are similar, irrespective of the taxonomic group or the region and lies between 0.1-0.2.

On a contrary, when such an analysis is done amongst large areas, like continents, the slope of regression would be much steeper with value of 0.6-1.2.

Question 5 What are the major causes of species losses in a geographical region?

Sol. The major causes of species losses in a geographical region are
(i) habitat loss and fragmentation.
(ii) over-exploitation of natural resources.
(iii) alien species invasions
(iv) co-extinctions
(v) pollution
(vi) Intensive agriculture
(vii) Hunting and forest fire

Question 6 How is biodiversity important for ecosystem functioning?

Sol. Biodiversity plays a major role in many ecosystem services that nature provides, which are as follows
(i) **Pure oxygen** The Amazon forest is estimated to produce, through photosynthesis, 20% of the total oxygen in the earth's atmosphere.
(ii) **Pollination** without which plants cannot give us fruits or seeds, is another service, ecosystems provide through pollinators - butterflies, bees, bumblebees, birds and bats.
(iii) **Flood and soil erosion control** plants help water retention, percolation and prevent soil erosion.
(iv) **Nutrient replenishment** plant biomass that falls on ground is the biggest source of recycled nutrients after decomposition.
(v) Waste recycling by microbes and other insects, etc., without which the Earth would simply become a huge pile of garbage and polluting material.
(vi) **Aesthetic pleasure** that we derive from nature, by walking through thick woods, watching spring flowers in full bloom or waking up to a bulbul's song in the morning.

Question 7 What are sacred groves? What is their role in conservation?

Sol. Sacred groves are sacred tracts of forest that are held in high esteem by local communities.

They are protected by local communities through social traditions and taboos that incorporate spiritual and ecological values.

Sacred groves are the most undisturbed forest patches and are thus, rich in biodiversity and harbour many rare species of plants and animals.

Such sacred groves are found in Meghalaya (Khasi and Jaintia hills), Aravalli hills of Rajasthan, Western Ghats, regions of Karnataka and Maharashtra and Madhya Pradesh (Bastar, Chanda and Sarguja region).

These regions are free from all types of exploitation and many have rare and endangered species.

Question 8 Among the ecosystem services are control of floods and soil erosion. How is this achieved by the biotic components of the ecosystem?

Sol. Flood and soil erosion is controlled by plants with the help of its roots. The roots bind to the soil firmly and thus prevent soil erosion by wind or water. The water that comes down as rain does not hit the forest floor directly, it first hits the tree tops and then slowly pass down into the forest floor. This reduces the chances of collection and stagnation of water and hence prevents floods.

Question 9 The species diversity of plants (22%) is much less than that of animals (72%). What could be the explanations to how animals achieved greater diversification?

Sol. Animals are mobile so they can migrate to other regions to escape stressful and harsh conditions or simply to explore new pastures. Their area of exploration is much larger and therefore have greater diversity.

Question 10 Can you think of a situation, where we deliberately want to make a species extinct? How would you justify it?

Sol. Humans can cause extinction of species through various means. The small pox virus (*Variola*) has been successfully eradicated through a campaign of the WHO that involved mass vaccination. If some microbes are dangerous to human society and other than having a parasitic interaction, do not serve any useful purpose, then such an attempt is justified.

DIKSHA APP *Questions*

☐ Short Answer Type

Q.1 Acccording to IUCN 2004 estimates we only know about 1.5 million species of plants and animals and according to Rays estimate the actual global species diversity could be about 7 million. If we have such a large biological diversity still why do biologists feel we need to conserve biodiversity explain?

Sol. We need to conserve the biodiversity because biodiversity helps to maintain the balance and heal ecosystem, supports human needs and well-being. All the species are interconnected through trophic levels it means that the extinction of one can have cascading effects throughout the ecosystem. This can disrupt food chains, alter nutrient cycles, and impact the stability of the entire system.

For instance, if a predator species goes extinct, its prey may overpopulate, leading to vegetation depletion and affecting other species dependent on that vegetation. This interdependence highlights the ultimate importance of preserving biodiversity to maintain ecosystem balance and functionality.

Q.2 How is the 'sixth extinction' presently in progress different from the previous episodes?

Sol. Since the origin and diversification of earth there were five episodes of mass extinction of species. However the 'sixth extinction' takes place rapidly. The current species extinction rates are estimated to be 100 to 1,000 times faster than in the pre-human times. Human activities such as deforestation, industrialisation, etc are responsible for this extinction. Ecologists warn that if the present trends continue, at the same rate then, nearly half of all the species on earth might be wiped out within the next 100 years.

☐ Long Answer Type

Q.1 (a) What are endangered species and how they are different from rare species?

(b) What are the different causes of accelerated rates of species extinction the world is facing?

Sol. (a) **Endangered species,** are at risk of extinction because of a sudden rapid decrease in its population or a loss of its critical habitat. *eg.* red panda is an endangered animal.

Rare species, involves group of organisms that are very uncommon, scarce, or limited in geographical areas *e.g.,* Himalayan brown bear.

(b) The accelerated rates of species extinctions that the world is facing now are largely due to human activities. There are four major causes, The Evil Quartet is the sobriquent used to describe them .

- **Habitat loss and fragmentation** This is the most important cause driving animals and plants to extinction.
- **Over-explloitation** It refers to the excessive use or extraction of natural resources beyond their sustainable limits. It can result in habitat loss, reduced biodiversity and increased carbon emissions.
- **Alien species invasions** When alien species are introduced unintentionally or deliberately, some of them turn invasive, and cause decline or extinction of indigenous species.
- **Co-extinctions** When species becomes extinct, the plant and animal species, which are closely associated with it in an obligatory way also become extinct.

www.ingramcontent.com/pod-product-compliance
Lightning Source LLC
Chambersburg PA
CBHW060923140726
47996CB00001B/361